The Story
of
The Cross

Foreword by
Harold P. Barker

F. A. Perigo

JOHN RITCHIE LTD
CHRISTIAN PUBLICATIONS

40 Beansburn, Kilmarnock, Scotland

ISBN-13: 978 1 909803 76 3

Copyright © 2014 by John Ritchie Ltd.
40 Beansburn, Kilmarnock, Scotland

www.ritchiechristianmedia.co.uk

Typeset by John Ritchie Ltd., Kilmarnock
Printed by Bell & Bain Ltd., Glasgow

THE STORY OF THE CROSS

FOREWORD

ANYONE who helps to give the Cross a central place in our thoughts is indeed a contributor to our spiritual welfare. And it is this that Mr. Perigo sets out to do in the book that the reader holds in his hands.

The Cross is being relegated to a back place in the popular religion of to-day. I say " religion," and not " Christianity," for nothing can be called Christianity that is not based on the Cross. In many quarters its meaning is perverted ; it is made to differ only in degree from the crosses on which hundreds of Christ's servants have met their death, honoured to resemble their Master in this, but never forsaken by God, never made the Sin-bearer for others, never shedding one drop of *atoning* blood.

But the Cross has a far-reaching significance, and to its many aspects our author calls our attention.

May we not, each one, write a brief Chapter 15, heading it " The Sinner who Received the Saviour," and weaving into it the story which is true of ourselves ? For this book will make its special appeal to those who know *experimentally* something of the deeper meaning of the Cross.

H. P. BARKER.

CONTENTS

———

CHAPTER I.

JUDAS, WHO BETRAYED THE SAVIOUR.

" Jesus said unto him, Judas, betrayest thou the
Son of Man with a kiss ? "

—Luke 22 48.

TWENTY-THREE miles south of Jerusalem
in a direct line, there nestled some hamlets
containing farm houses which came within
the lot of Judah when the land was distributed
to the twelve tribes during the days of Joshua.
These hamlets forming a large village, was
called Kerioth, and is mentioned once only
in Scripture (namely, Joshua 15. 25), and is
not to be confused with Kerioth in Moab,
which is mentioned three times in Scripture.
This Kerioth south of Jerusalem is exactly
seven miles from Hebron, and here it was
in this peaceful village that a boy was born
named Judah, at the beginning of the Christian era.

As he grew up, this boy, probably through
his parent's fear of the Roman Invader,
altered his name to Judas, which is the
Roman equivalent to Judah, and the word

Kerioth was altered to Iscariot. No doubt Judas in his boyhood days had many privileges which we may take for granted, as naturally he seemed to slip into the role of cashier to the heavenly band of Christ's disciples, for whoever has heard of an uneducated man handling money with all its implications without education, even though in this case it would only be that Judas would be the custodian of cash belonging to the eleven disciples and a few women.

We may therefore judge without controversy that Judas was attractive, educated and plausible. This may be strengthened by considering the testing time of the Passover Supper, for there when the Saviour said " One of you shall betray me " there was no suspicious look at Judas ; rather they suspected themselves, which suggests that he still further put on another cloak—that of piety.

Such was the man who grew up from boyhood with the greatest privilege that has ever been given to any person ever born, namely :—to be a companion of Jesus. But as Scripture is silent in regard of the early days of Judas, we do well not to trespass into the fields of speculation especially as it is the desire of the writer to cleave very closely to what is actually recorded lest harm might result from straying into by-path meadow.

Before, however, dealing with the dreadful crime which has stamped upon the whole face of the world the name " Judas " as representing something for which no language can adequately express, we will first simply deal with one or two incidents in his association with the Saviour.

First we find that he is numbered with the eleven disciples and is mentioned last in such numbering. (See Luke 6. 16, being called there " the traitor.") Here it must be noted that he is mentioned last not as an oversight, but because the Lord Jesus was so commanded by His Father, in that chapter. This may be gathered from the fact that in verse 12 Jesus goes into a mountain to pray and continues all night in prayer to God, and of course that communion would result in receiving counsel for the work He had to do. And so it was the privilege of Judas to be numbered amongst the disciples of Jesus, and was one of the twelve whom our Lord had chosen to be always with.

He was the intimate friend and acquaintance of the pure minded John—of the ardent, warm-hearted Peter—of the upright, honourable James—and the daily associate of the delightful, simple-minded, single-hearted others, whom also as we shall find he sought to carry away with him from their allegiance to the Master. Beyond all this wonderful companionship, he enjoyed, during the three and a half years ministry of Christ, the society of Jesus, who was the world's greatest Benefactor in His ministry on earth as well as the Saviour of sinners in His ministry on the Cross.

This privilege of companionship was extended to hearing the discourse in public of Christ as well as the private talks to His own—He was honoured with His more peculiar and confidential intercourses in private— he was privileged to be present when Jesus prayed (which so struck the other disciples that they said, " Lord teach us to pray like that "—Luke 11. 1) —he witnessed almost all the miracles which Jesus performed and so had every opportunity of forming a correct estimate of the character of his Master. During the three years of his companionship he was entrusted with great marvellous gifts, for in common with the other disciples he travelled more than once through Judea and Galilee preaching the kingdom of God, healing all manner of sickness amongst the people, and casting out demons.

With all the advantages and privileges

enjoyed by him, it is disturbing to think that he had one besetting sin, which was that of greed—greed of money. Notwithstanding his association for three years with the purest, loveliest Person, and of whom it was written one thousand years before He comes that He should be " the fairest of ten thousand and the altogether Lovely One," whose kindness and benevolence shows in all He said and did, wretched Judas appreciated none of His kindness ; love of money caused him to catch none of the nobleness of mind which distinguished his Master.

His mind was so set on the love of money, that the Blessed Christ of God did not once make use of his services as cashier, at least there is no record of His so doing, for when the opposers of Christ say " Is it lawful to give tribute to Caesar or not " (Luke 20. 22) He does not turn to Judas, but says to them " Show me a penny," and this together with the other incident when the opposers say to Peter (Matt. 17. 24-28) " Does not your Master pay tribute," we read that Peter was intercepted by Jesus on his way to the house where presumably Judas was, to ask him for the necessary money, and instead of this Christ performed a miracle which we may think suggests that Judas was to be left severely alone to his idol—the love of money.

This greed for gold became stronger, in fact it became an obsession, and when the Blessed Lord was anointed by Mary at the supper given to Him at Bethany a few days before the last Passover Supper his indignation was aroused and he said it could have been sold for two hundred pence and given to the poor, not that he cared for the poor, we read, but "because he was a thief and had the bag." Judas thus was forming habits which prepared him for the perpetration of the vilest deed that has ever disgraced humanity when he betrayed his Master for a sum of money which is less than £3 10s. 0d. of present English coinage.

Mention has already been made that he had influenced the others for evil and this is observed when in the house of Simon the leper (Matthew 26. 6-13). The disciples had indignation we are told over the presumed waste of ointment. Simon's house might be the one referred to in the previous incident, but as Scripture is silent we are not entitled to be speculative and therefore we must leave the matter.

What a lesson all this teaches us as we follow this man on his way to the palace of the High Priest and stand with him as he reveals his dark designs and covenants to receive the wages of iniquity, afterwards with his Master at the memorable Last Supper. And now the Pass-over Supper is ending and Jesus we read is "troubled in spirit" (John 13. 21). He is to suffer.

For He, unlike every other person in the world, knew in advance what is to take place. In a few hours, He knew that He would have to meet Satan in the garden of Gethsemane once more—for having bound the strong man in the wilderness in the beginning of His ministry and having taken away his goods by liberating souls from disease and death and demon, the devil is about to come again in person at the end of His public ministry to turn Him aside from His great atoning sacrifice for sin.

This Holy, sinless Person, reviews at the Passover Supper all that is shortly to take place, for not only is there betrayal by one, denial by another, the forsaking of all the disciples ;—He was to experience the weight of darkness, the unutterable anguish of spirit, the mocking, the scourging— and, finally, in the darkness, for His God to withdraw from Him, and all this lies upon His holy spirit. As to whether Judas was present at the Supper of Remembrance is open to question, but certain it was that he was present on the Thursday evening during the Passover Supper which was the day following the Wednesday when he had made the agreement with the Chief Priests. Judas retires from the presence of matchless goodness personified in the person of his Master, for we read that after the sop (John 13. 27) Satan entered into him. And in verse 30 we read that he received the sop and went " immediately out and it was night " !

On the eastern side of Jerusalem the bank slopes down to the Brook Kedron, and on the other side of the stream rises the Mount of Olives at the foot of which is a garden called Gethsemane which derives its name from the fact that it was here that olives were pressed out.

We cannot read the workings of the mind of Judas, but it is quite possible that having caused the other disciples to agree with him as to the alleged waste in the house of Simon the leper, Judas determines to secure some money for his own personal services for he would appear to have gone directly from the house of Simon to the palace of the High Priest and it is possible that in taking this step, greed was quickened by resentment at the apparent waste. Be that as it may, we follow Judas.

It was the time of the full moon, and now Levitical police of the temple with staves, and a number of Roman soldiers, under officers armed with swords, together with camp followers carrying lanterns to illuminate the way and doubtless some of the members of the Sanhedrin (eager to see that the design of arresting Christ should not miscarry) are drawing near. All these were furnished with lanterns to guide the feet and torches to light up the road, probably because in their ignorance they thought they might have to hunt for Jesus and His followers. It is dreadful to think that Judas could not only have violated the sanctuary of his Master, for we read that Gethsemane was a favourite resort of Jesus, but it would appear that the crowning act of his treachery was the sign by which he agreed to make his Master known to His enemies.

Coming near to the Garden, Judas hurries forward as if to warn Him of His danger and he flung himself on His neck sobbing " Master, Master." This kiss of Judas was the sign of discipleship, for in the East students used to kiss their Rabbis, and it is possible that this was the custom between Christ and His disciples. Even in our day, as soon as we become His disciples we may be said to kiss Him and every time we remember the Lord in His supper of remembrance we renew the pledge of our loyalty to Him which thus becomes a weekly challenge to our affections. It has been said by another that "in our baptism as believers He may be said to take us up in His arms and kiss us whilst in the supper of remembrance we return this mark of affection."

Returning to Judas, it is quite possible that he, being a guide (as observed by Peter in Acts 1. 16), would be walking ahead and probably retired into the shadows away from the moonlight ; but now this mean crowd who had employed the traitor as their guide were surprised by the Lord coming forward with the question "Whom seek ye," and they were so startled that they fell backwards to the ground for He was completely Master of the situation. They were "startled," because this was the evidence of impotence in the presence of Omnipotence. The "I Am" of eternity stepped forth. His closing words "this is your *hour* and the power of darkness" strikes at the very root of the activity of evil for it says in effect :—This midnight hour is your hour because you are sons of the night. (What a contrast, thank God, to know that true believers are sons of the day and therefore have nothing secret of which they need be ashamed.) "Your hour" to understand this it is necessary to study carefully John 7. 30 ;

8. 20 ; 12. 27 ; 13. 1 ; 17. 1. God answers Satan's hour of challenge by allowing His Son to step forth in atoning suffering.

Now we find that Judas, no longer a disciple but a traitor, moves along with the crowd to the palace of Caiaphas the high priest and when in the morning he learns that the chief priests and elders of the people have taken counsel against Jesus to put Him to death and after binding Him, He is delivered to Pontius Pilate, the Governor :— then it is that Judas sees that Jesus is condemned. Conviction flashes upon his conscience and sorrow fills his heart, and whereas before he can only think of his gain now he can only remember his crime and can only think of trying to undo what he had done. He brings the thirty pieces of silver to the Elders saying " I have sinned in that I have betrayed innocent blood," only to receive from his co-partners in crime their callous reply " What is that to us, see thou to that." Filled with remorse he throws the money down and he hanged himself.

Here we may contrast the remorse of Judas with the repentance of Peter. Judas never called Jesus " Lord " because he was a lip believer only, but time and again Peter called his Master " Lord," and whilst we read " The sorrow of the world worketh death " (referring to Judas), the apostle Paul says, pointing to Peter, " For godly sorrow worketh repentance unto salvation not to be repented of " (2 Cor. 7. 10).

A further lesson for our consideration may be in looking into the grievous fall of Judas. Money is not the root of all evil, it is the " *love* of money which is the root of all evil " (1 Tim. 6. 10). Under the guiding power of the Holy Spirit money can be most usefully used for the glory of God, but it becomes a very great snare unless prayer and the word of God are allied with it.

More sins have been committed through the craving of money than any other form of idolatry. This poor sinful world is suffering and sighing through the activities produced in its acquisition from its first introduction into the world. Nearly all the crimes and murders and sorrow attaching to this sin-stained scene are traceable to this love of money, and alas, more solemn still, souls are eternally lost, since its hold upon persons' minds is a vice-like grip. A special curse would appear to attach itself to the very word.

Indeed the true rendering of that solemn passage in 1 Timothy 6. 10 is " the love of money is the root of *every* evil." How often it is forgotten that there are no pockets in a shroud ! May we through special mercy from God be kept free from its hideous snare, for even true believers are sometimes scarred from the wounds it inflicts.

> Faithful amidst unfaithfulness,
> 'Mid darkness only light,
> Thou didst Thy Father's name confess
> And in His will delight.
>
> Unmoved by Satan's subtle wiles,
> Or suffering shame and loss,
> Thy path uncheered by earthly smiles
> Led only to the Cross.

CHAPTER II.

HEROD, WHO MOCKED THE SAVIOUR.

" And Herod with his men of war set Him at nought, and mocked Him, and arrayed Him in a gorgeous robe, and sent Him again to Pilate."
—Luke 23. 11.

THERE are several Herods mentioned in the New Testament. We must now determine which Herod it was of whom the Scripture of Truth speaks.

The first Herod was he who slew the babes of Bethlehem, when the infant Saviour was carried away to Egypt ; he was called Herod the Great, being born B.C. 73 ; he died from a dreadful disease shortly after his wicked act in slaying the Babes of Bethlehem, and at his death his dominions were divided between his sons by the Roman Conqueror. Judea was given to Archelaus, who was brother to the Herod of whom we are about to write ; but it was soon taken from him to be adminis-tered by the Romans themselves to the procurators, of whom Pilate was one. Galilee and its surroundings were given to another

22

son Antipas and a region more to the north given to a third son Philip.

Before we continue with the history of Herod Antipas we will mention in passing that the nephew of this Herod was the Herod Agrippa who slew the apostle James and tried to take Peter also, as narrated in the Acts of the Apostles, and was shortly afterwards, when in the act of receiving divine honours, as graphically narrated in the Antiquities of Josephus, smitten by the angel of death and expired, after a few days of excruciating agony. His great nephew was the Agrippa before whom Paul pleaded in the presence of Festus in Caesarea and whose voice has re-echoed down through the pages of history with the words " Almost thou persuadest me to be a Christian " (Acts 26. 28).

Herod Antipas was a man of considerable ability and at the beginning of his career he gave promise of becoming a good ruler. He had a passion for architecture and one of his achievements was the building of the city of Tiberius which is still well known in connection with modern missions ; but in the midst of his success he made a very serious moral lapse which proved fatal, for he entered into a vulgar intrigue with the wife of his own brother Philip, and when she left Philip to come to him bringing with her her daughter Salome, this weak king sent away his own wife, daughter of Aretas, who was the King of Petraea.

We mention this step proving "fatal," because, after the wicked crime of slaying John the Baptist in prison rather than break his promise, King Aretas, father of his discarded wife, seized an early opportunity to revenge his daughter's wrong and invaded the country, inflicting upon Herod an ignominious defeat.

It is interesting to observe the workings of conscience in this King Herod, for the language of Holy Scripture tells us that when John the Baptist commenced to fire the country with the flame of his mission, Herod took a great interest in his preaching, and invited him to the palace where he heard him gladly, until at last the uncompromising John tells him that it is not lawful to have his brother's wife. What an opportunity this was for Herod to adjust things, but, alas, he closes the door of repentance himself by putting John into prison and although for a time he threw around him the arm of protection his heart was not changed, and he remained in his sins. Thus we see that Satan catches Herod in his toils and then commenced to put the screw on.

It has been said by another that : "The commission of one sin is often like the opening of some vast flood gates or the breaking down of the embankment of some mighty river by which you are soon inundated and completely overwhelmed."

The test arrives, eagerly awaited by Satan. Herod celebrates his birthday by great feastings to his lords and high captains of Galilee, and, intoxicated with wine, he commands the daughter of Herodius to dance before him and his friends, which was reserved for the last as a special entertainment. This particular dance of Salome has intrigued the whole world and has been described as the "Dance of the Seven Veils," and it is understood that there are seven dances at the end of each of which some garment is discarded, leaving no garment at the seventh dance, which is calculated to fill the pure mind with disgust. This poor King feels so honoured at this shameless exhibition of a princess before his courtiers that he promises to give her whatever she might ask, even to the half of his kingdom, and when, instructed by her mother, she demands the head of John the Baptist it was not refused her. (See Mark 6. 17-28.)

What a privilege, we may add in passing, that we can say those words "Lead us not into temptation but deliver us from evil," for this involves that we have no strength of our own, but throws us upon the tender and loving grace of One who said at the end of His life, " Be of good cheer, I have overcome the world."

Now, in addition to his guilty sins, he has, to torment him, a guilty conscience, to drown which we are told that his court becomes distinguished for Roman imitations and affectations. Into his court he introduced singers, dancers, jugglers ; and the fibre of his character became so relaxed as to become a mere mass of pulp ready to receive every impression but ready to retain none ; he becomes less and less a man and is effeminate, so much so that Pontius Pilate breaks out in dislike and enmity in his disgust of this moral deterioration of this one time clever king.

So it is that after the prophet is murdered he immediately hears of the fame of Jesus, and, terror stricken, he cries out " This must be John the Baptist whom I have killed but is risen from the dead, and therefore mighty works do show forth themselves in him."

We read that Herod was exceeding glad to see Him, and this for two reasons. One was that Pilate and he became friends again, and the other was he was hoping that some miracle would be done by Him ; and so Herod questioned Him in many words, but Jesus answered Him not. It is not a little significant that the Saviour should be silent and we may take it that Christ will always be silent to those who live only for pleasure. Many go to churches to be amused or as a matter of convention, but they must certainly come away empty. They do not mind ritual or music, but let Christ be mentioned as being the need for the soul by the earnest preacher and the appeal only falls upon deaf ears. God will never gratify curiosity but He certainly will hear the cry of need, whilst the door of repentance is still open.

And so, having a mission given Him by His Father, we may say it was morally impossible for the Lord Jesus to exert His power of healing for the amusement of a vain and wicked man ; the silence of our Lord was in perfect harmony with the dignity of His person and the nature of His works. We may take it that the remorse of Herod on account of the murder of John had in a great measure died away, and so in his great desire to see Jesus and to hear Him speak he was influenced by curiosity only. The opportunities Herod had of knowing the truth had been neglected by him and he is finally given up to himself and to his sins.

God says, as it were, " Let him alone," and thus the Saviour of sinners never spoke to Herod of the murder of John or attempted to alarm his conscience or awaken his fears, but told him nothing, and in this profound silence we find it is the silence of heaven itself. How solemn !

Let us consider the treatment which our Lord receives at the hands of Herod. When Herod found that this Prisoner declined to answer any of his questions he treated Him with the greatest contempt and indignity. Regarding Him as of no account, for we read " He set Him at nought," he allows his men-of-war to treat Him with ridicule, and, mocking Him, we read that He was arrayed, probably by Herod himself, in a gorgeous robe which was most likely in imitation of the white robe worn at Rome by candidates for office and thereby suggests that Jesus offered himself as candidate for the throne of the country ; this robe would be kept by Herod.

What a cruel joke, because this dignified Prisoner would be driven out of the presence of Herod with shouts of laughter, mockery and contempt. And this is man ! The high office of Herod alone should have protected

Him against such brutal, shabby treatment. How extraordinarily like Pilate—as we shall see later ; Herod admitted the innocence of Christ and yet he treated Him with the grossest brutality.

The final opportunity given to Herod was now lost for all time—that of throwing around Him the shield of his protection. Herod must have known without any shadow of doubt of the innocence of the Saviour, since the greater part of His public life was spent in Galilee (Herod's dominions) and the greater part of the disciples themselves were Galileans.

So that if His preaching and His conduct had been seditious, Herod must certainly have known it, and even now, when the Chief Priests and Scribes stood and vehemently accused Christ, the testimony from the lips of Pilate (Luke 23. 15) is :—" No, nor yet Herod ; for I sent you to him, and lo, nothing worthy of death is done unto Him." If, in the case of Judas, " what think ye of Christ," the answer was " the love of money which is the root of every evil," in Herod's case " friendship with the world " weighed heavily in the scales against " what think ye of Christ."

Every person since Christ has come on the scene will have to answer this question for himself, by accepting Him, either during his or her lifetime, or it will be answered for us afterwards ; in eternal woe !

It may be well to suggest what may have led up to this rupture between Herod and Pilate. We gather from our opening remarks that Pilate despised the effeminate King, but this enmity may have been strengthened by the incident narrated by Christ himself during the days of His public ministry :— the destruction of the Galileans " whose blood Pilate mingled with their sacrifices." Permit now a personal enquiry. Gentle reader, does Christ speak no more to you ? I do not refer to religious excitement, your prayers night and morning which may be sincere, your private Bible reading which may or may not be a duty with you, your acts of courtesy to the poor, which send a thrill through your very being, being kind to others. I do sincerely ask if you seek His company for Himself alone, for that is the acid test. Even in earthly relationships it is a well-known fact that we hasten to get into the presence of one we love that we might interchange thoughts, and speak familiarly, confidentially, privately, with one another. Even in the busy world around us we have the quiet retreat of happy domestic life, the loving look of the wife to the husband, the husband to the wife, the mother to tha child, the proud father to his clever son. All this, which impresses the eye and the heart, but faintly illustrates the present speaking of Christ to His own.

In that memorable tenth chapter of John we have these never-to-be-forgotten words "My sheep hear my voice and they follow me," and again we read "A stranger will they not follow for they know not the voice of strangers."

To a happy believer his loss could never be replaced did a day go by without hearing his Master's voice speaking to him and he himself responding, for occupation with Christ is the secret of a happy life. If you, dear reader, do not experience this happy communion, then your loss is loss indeed, and you are truly walking in darkness with your feet liable to stumble at any moment. Be it remembered that the silence of our Lord in the presence of Herod is in strict accord with the retributive character of divine principles. Herod had had many opportunities of knowing the truth and these he had neglected in addition to which he had murdered God's messenger John the Baptist, and also, since every man has to reap what he sows in the flesh, we have the solemn words " Because I called and you refused,

I stretched out my hand and no man regarded,
therefore I will mock at your calamity, and
will laugh when your fear cometh." (Proverbs 1. 24-26.)

Nought, nought, I count as pleasure,
   Compared, O Christ, with Thee !
Thy sorrow, without measure,
   Earned peace and joy for me.
I love to own, Lord Jesus,
   Thy claims o'er me divine,
Bought with Thy Blood most precious,
   Whose can I be but Thine.

O worldly pomp and glory,
   Your charms are spread in vain !
I've heard a sweeter glory,
   I've found a truer gain !
Where Christ a place prepareth,
   There is my loved abode ;
There shall I gaze on Jesus :
   There shall I dwell with God.

CHAPTER III.

PILATE WHO CONDEMNED THE SAVIOUR.

" And so Pilate, willing to content the people, released Barabbas unto them and delivered Jesus, when he had scourged Him, to be crucified."

—Mark 15. 15.

OF all the characters connected with the crucifixion of our Lord one person stands out above the rest and that is Pontius Pilate, who became His judge and condemned Him. Pilate has often been considered as a heartless, inhuman judge, and that he was cruel and ruthless. Cruel he certainly was, as his was the order to slay the Galileans at their feast, when we are told his soldiers disguised themselves by putting white garments over their weapons and when suspicions were allayed they slew them ; also he was unprincipled in his general conduct to serve ulterior motives, a striking example of which we have in his condemnation of our Lord, for he not only pronounced an unjust sentence, but he did so knowing it to be unjust, and

C

the ulterior motive lies in the fact that his secret ambition was to retain the friendship of Caesar.

It is interesting to find that before he suffered total shipwreck a loving hand was stretched out to save him—that of his wife, who had a dream, and sent to him in haste to urge him to have nothing to do with the Prisoner, and as a result of this warning Pilate was now in a state of mental distress amounting to agony, and he made again and again the most strenuous efforts to release the Redeemer. We have no doubt that the hand of God was in this dream, since it was a hand stretched out in love to save Pilate from his doom, to which he was fast hastening.

Pilate was a very astute man and it is pretty obvious that he possessed suitable qualifications for his high office. If we study carefully his enquiries during the trial, along with which he would not be ignorant of information previously received of the Blessed Saviour's ministry and miracles and the nature of His services, we find him quickly summing up the bitter enmity of the Scribes and Pharisees which is confirmed by those words " For he knew that the chief priests had delivered him for envy." (Mark 15. 10.) Pilate, therefore, whilst he does not appear to have understood our Lord's real character or to have known the precise nature of His claims, had a most complete conviction that the charges preferred against Him by the Jews were groundless, and in the face of the world he states " I find no fault in this man," and time and again he sought to release Him.

It was just at this time in his dilemma Pilate sees another hand stretched out to him and he seizes it eagerly thinking that it was about to save him ; this was the hand of the mob at Jerusalem. We read from the divine records that it was the custom of the Roman Governor on the Passover morning to release a prisoner to the people. Pilate embraces this opportunity and in so doing thought he saw a way of escape from his present disturbance of mind. A man is brought forward called Barabbas, meaning " son of the father," along with Jesus, and Pilate offers to the people their choice. This temptation was a very subtle one to the Jews, as, apart from the Roman yoke, the Scribes themselves in their laws and precepts distorted all that Jehovah had, through Moses His servant, given to them as laws, by adding laws of their own.

The people therefore had now an opportunity to answer the proud haughty Scribes,

Pharisees and Priests by releasing the Saviour, but the Chief Priests and Elders persuaded the multitude that they should ask for Barabbas and destroy Jesus, and their will prevailed, and so from ten thousand throats the cry came, "Not this man, but Barabbas." Thinking that it would appease the people, he ordered Jesus to be scourged by his soldiers, and so He—who in the high priest's palace was spit upon and struck in the face; and the soldiers covering up His face saying "Prophesy, O Christ, and tell us who smote Thee"—was now to be scourged. In the language of another we are told, "It took place, it would appear, on the platform where the trial had been held and in the eyes of all. The victim was stripped and stretched against a pillar or bent over a low post, his hands being tied so that He had no means of defending himself. The instrument of torture was a sort of knout, or cat o' nine tails with bits of bone or iron attached to the ends of the thongs. Not only did the blows cut the skin and draw blood, but not infrequently the victim died in the midst of the operation." All this Jesus suffered.

Some have suggested that Pilate, out of consideration for Jesus, may have moderated either the number or the severity of the strokes ; but on the other hand his plan of releasing Him depended on his being able to show the Jews that He had suffered severely. The inability of Jesus to bear His own cross to the place of execution was no doubt due to the exhaustion produced by this infliction ; which perhaps is a better indication of the degree of severity than mere conjecture.

After the scourging the soldiers took Him away with them to their own quarters in the palace, and called together the whole band to enjoy the spectacle. Evidently they thought that He was already condemned to be crucified ; for anyone condemned to crucifixion had, after being scourged, to be handed over to the soldiery to be handled as they pleased, just as a hunted creature when it is caught is flung to the dogs.

This was all in accordance with the laws of the Romans. And now for the Roman idea of a joke.

Stripping their august Prisoner they arrayed Him in an old purple robe (no doubt rejected by Pilate and handed over to a subordinate officer, and in this connection one can imagine Lydia, " a seller of purple," as mentioned in the Acts of the Apostles, shedding a few tears when the great apostle Paul would refer to that during his service in Philippi, for she came from Thyatira, a city devoted to the dyeing of garments with this imperial colour). This purple robe, probably torn and tattered, suggested a crown, and so from a thorn bush in the palace grounds one of the soldiers tore off a branch and weaving it into a rough crown placed it on His head.

It has been the writer's privilege to see a replica of this thorn bush and he has seen these thorns more than six inches long! The indignity of the Saviour continues, and in addition to His bleeding back, His head pierced by the thorns commenced also to bleed, and so He must bear the curse of the earth before the supreme one of bearing the curse due to sin. Then another soldier snatches up a bullrush reed and as a mock symbol of authority places this weak reed, about the strength of thin cardboard, used by shepherds as a whistling flute, into His right hand.

And so the King was dressed up, thus completing the Roman idea of a joke.—One can well understand how the great apostle Paul in writing to the Ephesians linking it up with those grosser sins which weigh man's soul down to perdition when he says (Ephesians 5. 3, 4) : " But fornication and all uncleanness or coveteousness let it not once

be named among you as it becometh saints,
neither filthiness nor foolish talking nor
jesting," and sternly thinking of the Saviour's
suffering on this occasion, he adds in verse 6 :
" Because of these things cometh the wrath
of God upon the children of disobedience."—
Then it is in mockery that one by one they
bend the knee to Him, imitating the courtiers
and senior officers in Caesar's army, but
exchange the words of " Ave Caesar " to
that of " King of the Jews." Then there is
a hush, for Pilate is re-entering the room
and the soldiers step back.

When Pilate sees his prisoner thus arrayed
he thought that it might appeal to the mob
outside, and so he takes this patient Sufferer
out with him on the balcony wearing the
crown of thorns and the purple robe ; but
the chief priests cry out again and again
" Crucify Him, crucify Him." And now
another factor in the case is striking terror
to the heart of Pilate :—they say " He
calls Himself the Son of God."

So Pilate, inwardly terror-stricken at the
thought of condemning One who was not
only a Righteous Man but some mysterious
person calling Himself the Son of God,
returned to the judgment hall and taking
Jesus with him asks " Whence art Thou,"
but Jesus gave him no answer as the many

warnings had been ignored by Pilate and the position was now hopeless. And now it is that the weak joint in Pilate's armour is revealed, for the Jews cry out " If thou let this Man go, thou art not Caesar's friend ; whoever maketh himself a King speaketh against Caesar." Pilate was now in a quandary because the Jews had found out his weak spot, and he decides to sit on the judgment seat in a place called the " Pavement " or a place called " the Gabbatha," and commands Jesus to be brought to the Praetorium or Judgment Hall.

The place called the " Pavement " appears to be an open space adjoining the Governor's palace on which a high stage was erected containing the seat which the Governor occupied in his judicious capacity surrounded by his guards and officers to administer justice on occasions when Jews could not enter into the house of a Gentile or expose themselves to the danger of touching anything that was unclean. It is here, therefore, that the trial of Jesus at the Roman Tribunal properly commences.

Pilate occupies the elevated seat of judgment surrounded by his officers and his guard. The chief priests and rulers and people stand in the open space below ; and Jesus is formerly arraigned.

Jesus stood before the Governor and they began to accuse Him, saying " We found this Fellow perverting the Nation and forbidding to give tribute to Caesar saying that He Himself is Christ a King." As He had already done in private, Jesus now publicly confessed to Pilate that He was the long expected King of the Jews. He astonished the Governor by not answering a word to the various accusations which the Jews brought against Him. Pilate rose from the judgment seat officially declaring his conviction of the innocence of Jesus, and as he was accustomed to release one prisoner to them at the feast he proposed to release the Redeemer. " But they were the more fierce, saying, He stirreth up the people teaching throughout all Jewry beginning from Galilee to this place." (Luke 23. 5.)

What an extraordinary position the Jews now find themselves in. In their religious law-keeping in order not to be defiled they refused to enter the judgment hall and so to meet them Pilate brings this Meek and Lowly One to Gabbatha outside where they may do their worst to this Lamb of God and still eat the Passover without being defiled. What a death blow to religion where it is an empty shell without Christ.

It was now nearly eight o'clock in the

morning, and weary with the hatred around him, Pilate cries out, "Shall I crucify your King," only to bring out the answer of men who had forsaken their God, "We have no King but Caesar." Pilate feared for the public peace knowing the tendency of the people with whom he had to deal, for now that their passions were wrought up even to the pitch of frenzy any further resistance might cause the cloud to burst and a storm to fall upon him for which he was not prepared. Then it was he feared an accusation against him and the consequence of it to Rome. Pilate knew that there were many other acts of his government which were oppressive, unjust and cruel, and he knew that these still rankled in the public mind and would be remembered against him along with any accusation. Pilate was aware that although in the darkest hour conscience would vindicate him in the acquittal of Jesus, neither to conscience nor to Tiberius Caesar could he justify those proceedings. Hence it is said that willing to content the people he delivered Jesus to be crucified so that, cost what it may, the unrighteous deed must be done. From this moment he is not a ruler of the people nor their master, but their servant and the slave of his own fears.

As to his personal blame, whilst we know

he was not the greatest sinner of all engaged in the dreadful transaction, yet he knew it was wrong and no man can violate his conscience without guilt.

And so in handing over Christ to the soldiers for crucifixion, he degraded his high office and he degraded himself.

Before we close his history, the last scene we see of him is that of a vain attempt even in the act of doing wrong to rid himself of the guilt of it, for we read in Matthew 27. 24 : " When Pilate saw that he could prevail nothing, but that rather a tumult was made, he took water, and washed his hands before the multitude, saying, ' I am innocent of the blood of this just person ; see ye to it.' "

His attempt, however, to rid himself of it by washing his hands was in vain. He was a guilty person and guilt has to be atoned for ; no water can wash that away, and the very thing that led to Pilate's downfall morally, became his downfall as to his high office.

Of necessity he had to record the crucifixion of Jesus with a short summary of its history to his master Tiberius in Rome, but when he received it, he immediately sent for Pilate to account for both that and other matters and he was banished in disgrace.

Travellers to-day tell us of a little island in the Mediterranean, and it is supposed that

Pilate was banished here. Two years afterwards, in remorse at the loss of his friendship with his master, this conscience-stricken man committed suicide, at a spot called Mount Pilatus on this island.

Here we may remark how very different was the Saviour's treatment of His dear friend John who was banished to Patmos sixty years afterwards, where he received revelations which thrill the heart of the reader to-day. We may ask what lesson we may learn from Pilate and his conduct, and in this connection we are told that " Whosoever will be a friend of the world is the enemy of God " (James 4. 4). This world system is with us still to-day, and in these winding-up moments of God's patience with the Gentiles we find that to-day is a day of decisions. Decisions first for Christ, then decisions in regard of loyalty to Him, a rejected absent Lord. Decisions as to service and all that it involves. Decisions to serve this Master in telling others about Him and serving Him amongst His people, which is the greatest test of all, although it is the greatest service.

For problems arise amongst the assemblies of God's people which call for tact, patience, wisdom, kindness, forgiveness and grace, and it is for us to decide whether the world is to claim us with its darkness, sin, misery and judgment to come, or Christ, and serving Him in happy freedom in the light, holiness, joy, and the glory which lies right ahead. May our decision be for Him.

O Head! once full of bruises,
  So full of pain and scorn,
'Mid other sore abuses
  Mocked with a crown of thorn ;
O Head! e'en now surrounded
  With brightest majesty,
In death once bowed and wounded,
  On the accursed tree.

Thou countenance transcendant !
  Thou life-creating sun !
To worlds on Thee dependent—
  Yet bruised and spit upon ;
O Lord ! what Thee tormented,
  Was our sin's heavy load,
We had the debt augmented,
  Which Thou didst pay in blood.

CHAPTER IV.

The Rulers Who Persecuted The Saviour.

" And the chief priests and scribes stood and vehemently accused Him."

—Luke 23. 10.

Right from the beginning of our Lord's public ministry he had opposed to Him as chief persecutors the Jewish priests and rulers with their schools of opinion, such as

1. Those who expounded the law and its precepts :—*The Scribes*.
2. Those who lived for nothing but tradition and ritual :—*The Pharisees*.
3. Those who were so poisoned in their minds by Satan as not to believe in a future state or condition :—*The Sadducees*.

We have dealt with the betrayal of Judas, the weakness of Herod and the unworthiness of Pilate as a judge ; in subsequent chapters we shall hope to deal with the denial of Peter, the desertion of the apostles, the conduct of the executioners, and the attitude of the

malefactors who were crucified with Him :—
all to teach us to what depths humanity can
fall ; but it is scarcely possible for our fallen
humanity to be reduced to a more depraved
or obdurate state than that of the chief
priests and rulers who at every step opposed
the Saviour. There does not seem one re-
deeming feature with them, so much so
that Christ himself on many occasions was
indignant, and finally called them " a genera-
tion of vipers." Right through their conduct
is woven a thick strand of hypocrisy, and to
attempt to give even a pen picture of their
conduct towards the Blessed Saviour causes
the pen to tremble lest we be carried away
by feelings of indignation. Only the fact
that we are men of like passions makes us
tremble lest we fall into the same snare.

The history of these men is most humiliating in the extreme, not only in the fearful,
wicked part they took in the transaction of
our Lord's crucifixion but in their opposition
to Him at every step He took and with
every breath He drew. In their hostility
against the Light of the World they were
dishonest, and there does not seem a spark
of humanity in their hatred of the One who
had come especially from Heaven not to
judge the world but to save it.

There is no sincerity in the complaints

which they made respecting the so-called blasphemy of our Lord, for they did not in their consciences believe in the charges preferred against Him and upon which they procured His condemnation and death.

It is on this account, indeed, that the conduct of the Jewish priests and rulers is affecting and instructive as showing the fearful depths to which man can descend in dishonesty. We use the word "instructive" because we are describing a pen picture of religion without Christ and to show how it is possible for persons to think themselves good men, just rulers, labourers for the public weal, and at the same time to oppress and persecute the innocent even to stripes and death, robbing the righteous of honour and of life itself on charges which in their conscience they knew to be false ; yet extraordinary to say, their zeal was such that they would have died for the honour of their religion. We will now look at some of the features of their dishonesty.

Passing over the public ministry of the Lord Jesus which is summed up in one verse wherein it is stated in Hebrews that "He endured the contradiction of sinners against Himself," it seems pretty evident that their hostility originated in the success of His ministry and the increase of His influence,

48

and this had the effect of stimulating their malignity, thus reaching a climax in the resurrection of Lazarus. It may be well to outline four avenues of approach on the part of Satan to them which caused them to act as they did to the Redeemer.

1. *Their dishonesty.*
2. *The cause of their hostility.*
3. *The pretexts they used.*
4. *Their superstition with its attendant wickedness.*

1. *Their Dishonesty.* From the very first, these Scribes and Pharisees and religious leaders of the nation became bitter in their hostility when the searchlight of Heaven in the person of Christ shone upon their dark hearts and also lighted up their dark ways. There is, for instance, their attitude when the Saviour asked them on their own grounds a few days before the crucifixion, " The baptism of John whence was it from heaven or of man," and they reasoned within themselves and said, " If we say from heaven He will say why did ye not believe him, but if we say of man, we fear the people because all hold John as a prophet and they answered Him, we cannot tell." They were cornered, because they had actually sent messages to John to ask him who he was and had received his answer, but the fact

was they did not care to know because it
would mean altering their conduct and ways
together with their religious outlook.

A little later on their dishonesty is
accentuated still more by the manner in
which His trials were conducted.

Actually they would liked to have removed Him by private assassination, but
they feared the crowd ; and finally by craft
and subtlety they decided to murder Him,
not by violence but by procession of the law
to give it the legal flavour, and so in their
dishonesty they suborned false witnesses,
but none of these agreed with each other,
until one remembered that three and a half
years before this Saviour had said when
discoursing in the Temple, " Destroy this
Temple and in three days I will raise it again,"
and with the sanctimoniousness of the Pharisees and with all the gravity of judges they
condemned Him on this issue. When Jesus
refused to answer such a palpably dishonest
accusation they tried another plan—they
asked Him to tell them plainly if He were
Christ the Son of God or not. And to this
He answers, because it is the " voice of
adjuration " (see Leviticus 5. 1), and where
the person is silent that becomes a trespass ;
so the Saviour, true to His written word,
affirms the fact and adds, " Hereafter shall

ye see the Son of Man sitting on the right hand of power, and coming in the clouds of Heaven." This they were pleased to call :— blasphemy. When this new so-called crime fell to the ground they brought a new crime to his charge, the accusation being changed to that of sedition before Pilate. Pilate himself saw through this manoeuvre, and, moreover, knew that the Jews had delivered Jesus unto him out of envy.

Another proof of their dishonesty is seen in their treatment of Judas, for when he came to them and declared his own guilt and the innocence of Him whom he betrayed into their hands, they, the priests who should have been sympathetic, said callously and contemptuously to their co-partner in crime, " What is that to us, see *thou* to that."

Finally their dishonesty is clearly proved in their conduct to the Roman Guard. Soon after the crucifixion of the Prince of Glory these rulers recollected that Jesus had fore- told His resurrection from the dead on the third day. (We would remark here how strange that *they* should have remembered this when it had escaped the recollection of the apostles and all the brethren.) When in the recollection of this rising again they asked for a guard to seal the tomb and guard it, and when on the morning of the third day the body was missing, they (the guard) came to them with horror on every feature and trembling in every limb, declaring that they had seen an angel descend from Heaven, the brightness of whose appearance dazzled them and the majesty of whose look struck terror through their souls so that the guard swooned away and became as dead men. Then it was these rulers and chief priests covenanted to give these soldiers money to circulate one of the lamest falsehoods ever uttered by lying lips :—we marvel at the depths to which man can travel under the energising power of Satan.

These religious men excite our deepest detestation by the greatness of the dishonesty and the hardness of their hearts.

2. *The cause of their hostility.* We may ask, why did the chief priests and rulers act thus towards our Lord and seek His death by every possible means knowing that He was guilty of no crime ? Why was it that they could prefer Barabbas, a notorious criminal, before Jesus, the wise and holy Teacher full of goodness, the One who never turned any person away who might be in need ?

We have shown Judas to be a wicked man whose love of money sealed his doom ;

we have shown Herod who mocked Him, to be a slave of sin, and Pilate who condemned Him was utterly unprincipled as a judge; yet none of these hated Him or for a moment wished for His death; but these rulers will be satisfied with nothing short of His death—to contrive which they went to all lengths.

To find the cause of this we have to search their attitude towards our Lord, and we may say that the whole of the Saviour's conduct and ministry was in direct opposition to their views, their prejudices and their interests. In the first place their views were strictly and bitterly limited to the Jewish people and they had no time or place outside the nation. Certain it was that the chief priests and rulers looked for a great and powerful presence in the person of Messiah and they looked for national distinctions and honours during His reign, but first that He should free them from the Roman yoke. There was, however, nothing in the conduct or the ministry of the Blessed Saviour to favour these views; indeed His whole life may be summed up in these words, " The Son of Man came not to be ministered unto but to minister and to give His life a ransom for many."

There was much in their official position

and interests which rendered the Lord an object of constant suspicion ; and a bitter hatred for Christ, and His gentle, kind, loving ministry, was undermining their authority, so much so that they regarded Him as an enemy of the system to which they were devotedly attached. They could never forgive Christ and they pursued to the bitter end their hatred of all that was good and lovely and noble.

3. *The pretexts they used.* These men, dominated by Satan, would fain have men believe that their conduct had originated in zeal. There was indeed zeal for God, for the Law, for the Temple, for Moses, and, in the presence of Pilate, for Caesar and for the interests of the Roman Government. A zeal which found a second edition in the Middle Ages by persecuting bigots when they tortured prisoners and finally sent them to the stake. We have the sufferings of the Lollards, the Puritans, the Non-Conformists in our country ; the Waldenses, the Albigenses, the Huguenots on the Continent of Europe.

They took the law as their spring of conduct instead of Christ the Giver of the law, and so we get the remark, " Have any of the rulers or the pharisees believed of Him, but these people who knoweth not the Law are accursed." But it was quite true, as mentioned eight hundred years before, He was despised and rejected, "A Man of Sorrows and acquainted with grief, and we hid as it were our faces from Him." (Isa. 53.)

They were bitter against Christ because they were conscious of the fact that He had read their hearts.

4. *Their superstition and its attendant wickedness.* The simple beauty of sacred Scripture lies in the fact that it records facts simply, and the reader himself is to consider what principles they involve and what truths they teach under the guidance of the Holy Spirit. And so when we get these words recorded by the beloved Apostle John (18. 28), " Then led they Jesus from Caiaphas unto the hall of judgment ; and it was early ; and they themselves went not into the judgment hall lest they should be defiled ; but that they might eat the Passover ; " we pause and consider what it means. Here we see a set of men, pre-eminently religious, teachers, priests and rulers of the people, who are unquestionably above all others with religious privileges and all its advantages—in fact the Jewish people of God, men who are familiar with the Psalms of David and the writings of Isaiah, Jeremiah and other prophets. We see these men

55

pursuing their innocent victim to death, hesitating not to secure any expedient however wicked in order to obtain His destruction, challenging even high heaven in their fury, and yet when they come to the house of the Gentile in pursuit of their object, they stop on the threshold, for by entering therein they would become defiled! It might be asked, could a Jew never enter the house of a Gentile, and the answer is :—he could do so in ordinary circumstances, but he would expose himself to defilement, and if this be so it would require time and service in order to be cleansed.

If he were not cleansed he would not be allowed to participate in the service of the Temple or even enter its courts. The amazing thing, however, is revealed that outwardly they would not allow themselves to become defiled, but inwardly they were defiled by every form of wickedness and actually were about to wash their hands in the blood of innocence. Actually to have touched a heathen's garment that day would contract defilement, yet their conscience was such that it did not hinder them from wickedly pursuing to the death the Just One who came to be their Saviour.

Later on, having seen Him expire under murderous hands, they went back to the

Temple to enjoy a religious ordinance, with their prayers and their supplications, their hymns and commemorative psalms, their bread and cup of blessing, mingling with their congratulations to one another words of joy on the successful issue of their scheme of villainy.

Is it not that this was the last acceptable observance of the Jewish Passover as far as records go, for the age to which it belonged was about to pass away, and actually the light of a new dispensation was dawning upon the world. In the crucifixion of Christ the Jewish age had passed away for ever and the Jewish festival had become an unmeaning rite. They buried themselves in their own superstition.

May we not, as we read these lines, take stock of the situation and ask ourselves the question : " Are we still linked up with a superstitious religious world or are our lives bound up with a risen living Saviour who has abolished death and brought life and incorruptibility to light through the Gospel ? "

Lord, what is Man ? 'Tis He who died,
And all Thy nature glorified ;
Thy righteousness and grace displayed.
When He for sin atonement made ;
Obedient unto death, was slain—
Worthy is He o'er all to reign.

THE STORY OF THE CROSS.

Thy counsels e'er the world began,
All centred in the Son of Man ;
Him destined to the highest place,
Head of His church through sovereign grace,
To Him enthroned in Majesty
Let every creature bend the knee.

CHAPTER V.

THE SOLDIERS WHO CRUCIFIED THE SAVIOUR.

" And sitting down, they watched Him there."
—Matthew 27. 36.

WE have now reached a very solemn portion of our studies, that of the actual crucifixion of our adorable Saviour and Lord in relation to the soldiers who were the executioners. We have thought upon Gethsemane in our consideration of Judas and have dwelt upon Gabbatha in contemplating Pilate and his reaction, and now we are to view Golgotha and what it means.

Many people have been found to dilate upon the physical sufferings of our Lord, but the ground is so holy here that we would fear to tread even with un-shod feet, but for the fact that we believe the chief agony to Christ was not the physical sufferings or the moral effect upon His holy spirit at the treatment accorded Him by the crowds around the cross, but we believe that what His soul shrank from was the fact that He had to pay the awful price of atoning for sin.

Here it was at Golgotha that God had to deal with the question of sin in the person of Christ who came to be the Saviour of the world. His all atoning work avails for every man, woman and child who has ever trodden this earth.

Before the history of the Cross, everything looked forward to that stupendous event which we know as B.C. (before Christ).

In the period known as A.D. (anno domini in the year of our Lord) forgiveness is plenteous and free and it has been ordained in heaven that as a result of the work of Christ on the Cross, all classes of society, all ranks of men, should share in this transaction.

In passing it might be said, " Then if the work of Christ is for all and He has atoned for sin, surely every person is free and there is no such thing as not being forgiven." But the language of Holy Scripture is not so, and when the word of God states in Romans 3. 22 that the " righteousness of God by faith of Jesus Christ is into all," it says most emphatically " *upon* all them that believe " before it closes the verse. In other words, to be forgiven and consciously so, one has to accept it from God's hand as a free gift. And this is not all, for one has also to believe upon and own Christ as Lord the details of which may be seen in Romans 10. 9 and 10,

" That if thou shalt confess with thy mouth the Lord Jesus and shalt believe in thy heart that God hath raised Him from the dead thou shalt be saved. For with the heart man believeth unto righteousness and with the mouth confession is made unto salvation."

This is consistent with the full range of Scripture and in a word it might be said that salvation is based on two things, namely : —the word of God and the work of Christ. Coming back to the soldiers who crucified our Lord, these were not Jews but Romans, so that they had not the same grounds of opposition that the Jews had, and in one respect they were but fulfilling their Roman duty, and so, although they themselves were guilty of being the actual murderers of Jesus it was the priests and rulers who did not touch Him who were far more guilty of His murder than the soldiers who nailed Him to the Cross.

It will be remembered that Pilate washed his hands and delivered Jesus to be crucified after which the purple robe was taken off Him and his own garment placed on Him ; but He was still bound with cords, His back was bleeding and they had mocked Him and spit upon His face. Then they laid His Cross upon Him, but His strength after attempting to carry the Cross was not sufficient, and as time with the executioners became the essence of the contract they forced a person from the country to carry His Cross for Him, thus affording this strong man (as doubtless was Simon the Cyrenian) the greatest honour that has ever befallen any man on earth. Passing through the gate of Jerusalem there is, approximately a mile away, a tiny hill called Golgotha or Calvary where the first procession halted awaiting the procession of soldiers with the two thieves also carrying their crosses.

There were two forms of crosses in general use among the Romans ; one was a strong piece of timber crossed by a bar near the top in the form of a letter T, and the other cross would be two pieces of timber joined in the centre in the form of a letter X. We may gather that the cross of Christ was the first one, in the form of a letter T, because after the Saviour is suspended there, a superscription was written over His head by order of Pilate. He, as the central one, would be considered the greatest criminal and as such both His hands and His feet would be pierced by nails to the Cross, which would confirm the language of Psalm 22, " They pierced My hands and My feet."

With regard to the thieves, one on the right and one on the left, most probably they were bound to the crosses on which they were suspended and would thus escape much of the physical suffering endured by our Lord.

With what emotion the apostle Paul must have written those words in Colossians 2, 14. when he tells us what God has done, " Blotting out the handwriting of ordinances that was against us which was contrary to us and took it out of the way *nailing it to His cross.*"

We have remarked that these soldiers had no personal animosity to Christ for He had done nothing to provoke their hostility, but they were certainly guilty of much cruelty and brutality, as some of the band had previously stripped Him of His raiment, arrayed Him in the old purple robe, put the reed into His right hand as a mock sceptre, crowned Him with thorns, and in mockery cried " Hail, King of the Jews." Wretched sinful Roman soldiers to thus unite in insulting the most harmless Victim of oppression that ever lived, and thus they have clothed themselves with everlasting infamy by this wanton cruelty towards this meek and lowly Saviour.

And now, four soldiers, detailed off by the centurion to act as executioners, have the same brutality whilst He is on the Cross.

First we read that the soldiers also mocked Him offering Him vinegar (probably it was without the gall mixed with vinegar which would have the effect of stupifying the senses, but just sour wine). The vinegar mingled with gall was subsequently offered, but we read that, having tasted thereof, He would not drink, as He would appear in the presence of a holy God representing sinners, with unclouded mind. It was probably His very meekness and gentleness which caused resentment in their minds, as they could understand a person who is quick to resent an injury and act accordingly; but not so with this Divine Saviour, and having crucified Him, knowing that they had many hours to wait they sat down to wait for the end, having completed their task.

Little did the soldiers think that millions of angelic eyes were gazing upon this scene from heaven, that the destiny of worlds was bound up in this scene, and that countless multitudes of minds would be dwelling upon it when time shall be no more ; and little did they think that there would yet come a time when this One whom they pierced would be coming in the clouds of Heaven with power and with great glory. In ignorance they crucified the Son of God, the King of Glory. These soldiers were equally unconscious of the nature and grandeur of the transactions in which they were concerned.

Little did they think that they were so near to the Daysman between the injured and offended Governor of the universe and the apostate world, that the great Mediator of God's appointment for man's needs was then ministering before the Lord (His High Priestly office and work cannot, of course, be interrupted by death), and that He was then presenting the sacrifice which covered the guilt of the world, presenting an offering that would fill all Heaven with a fragrance that would never die, and shedding the blood which would wash away the deepest stains, the vilest pollution, which it did but touch. Little did they think that they were witnessing the greatest act of obedience to the Divine commands which God had ever received (" that mercy and truth met together," that " righteousness and peace embraced each other "), that sin was dealt with, man was saved, and God was glorified.

To these four soldiers belonged the garments of the Saviour which would fall to them as perquisites. And they at once proceeded to divide the spoil apart from the garment for the loins. There would be a large, loose upper garment, probably a head-dress, a girdle, a pair of sandals, and an under garment. This under garment was of one piece, and had probably been knitted for Him by the loving fingers of His mother, or one of the women who ministered to Him. These formed the entire property which Jesus had to leave and became the booty of the soldiers. This was the sole property of One who bequeathed the vastest legacy that has ever been left by anyone, large enough to enrich the whole world. Notorious for gambling, one finds a dice in his pocket and they gambled for His clothes, while the Son of Man is atoning for the sins of the world with angels and glorified spirits gazing down upon this scene of all scenes on this day of all days. The centurion who was in charge of the whole group of soldiers at this and the other crosses was tremendously impressed and stated " Truly this was the Son of God," after witnessing the upheaval of nature accompanying the sufferings and death of the central Victim. For his was a nobility of character enabling him to judge from a true perspective, but the soldiers themselves were sunk in a misery of vulgar sinfulness.

Then it was that, finally acting upon higher authority, it being the commencement of a Jewish high day, the centurion gives orders for them to be put to death. Probably the wooden mallet used to nail the hands and feet of the Blessed Saviour to the Cross of shame was picked up by one of the soldiers and he breaks the legs of the two thieves who were still alive, the shock to their nervous system producing death. Astonished upon coming to the central Cross to find that this One suspended there was already dead, one of them takes a spear, without which no Roman soldier is properly dressed, and pierced His side, so that two Scriptures could be fulfilled :—" A Bone of Him shall not be broken," leading us back fifteen hundred years before to Exodus 12. 46, and another Scripture :—" They shall look upon Him whom they pierced " (Zech. 12), the fulfilment of which is still future.

A few days later the risen Lord bids His disciples to go unto Jerusalem after they had received the Holy Ghost, and bids them in effect to search out the men who spit in His face, those who nailed Him to the Cross, those who insulted Him and who pierced His side, and say " There is forgiveness for *you*." Such is the grace of Christianity !

The horrible jest of the soldiers lies in the fact that after the centurion in charge received the superscription " King of the Jews " they said, " Very well, if He is a King He must have a guard of honour," and so, probably in hateful mockery the two thieves were placed on either side of Him and He in the midst.

In a coming day those who have been found faithful to Him in this the time of His rejection will be wonderfully honoured by being with Him as His guard of honour, for we are told that they that are with Him are " called and chosen and faithful." (Rev. 17. 14.)

May it be ours to covet that great privilege !

> There from His head, His hands, His feet,
>   Sorrow and love flowed mingled down.
> Did e'er such love and sorrow meet
>   Or thorns compose so rich a crown.
>
> Were the whole realm of nature ours,
>   That were an offering far too small ;
> Love that transcends our highest powers,
>   Demands our soul, our life, our all.

CHAPTER VI.

THE MALEFACTORS WHO SUFFERED WITH THE SAVIOUR.

" Then were there two thieves crucified with Him, one on the right hand and one on the left."
—Matthew 27. 38.

WHAT a sight this was, Jesus the innocent, spotless, sinless holy One, suffering and dying between two malefactors. Who would have thought, knowing and meditating upon His indefatigable service of love, unwearying in His seeking to serve others, of anticipating for Him such a death? Here were two criminals appointed to die that day and in the ordinary course of things would have been executed if Jesus had not been apprehended ; but as He also was condemned, He was executed with them.

Right through the whole of sacred Scripture where Jesus is shown it is always as in the centre or midst, as for instance in the Trinity we have God the Father, the *Son* and Holy Spirit ; in the midst of time in the six thousand years of the working out of this world's course of things, He appears on the

beginning of the fourth day, thus corresponding with Genesis 1, where the sun is
shown on the *fourth* day. In Revelation He
is shown as in the *midst* of the throne. In
the company of believers to-day He is true
to His word where there is affection for Him,
and in their gatherings He is in their midst,
and now in His death He is seen as in the
midst, crucified between two thieves. And
as if He were the vilest of them all this pre-
eminence was assigned Him in ignominy
and shame, truly in the vivid language of
the prophet Isaiah, " He was numbered
with the transgressors," which thus afforded
another proof of His Messiahship.

Let us consider the situation. Here are
three persons suffering at the same time
in the same place, the same cruel and ignominious death, and yet, how different in
point of character. Outwardly their form
was the same, inwardly there is not the
slightest resemblance between them. One
of those Persons is the most illustrious Being
that ever adorned our world—the Creator,
in fact, of it. Another is a sinner suffering
for his sins who eventually becomes, through
light entering his soul from God, penitent
in the spirit of his mind. The third one is a
profaned and hardened wretch, ripe for
destruction ; here we find heaven, earth and

hell in close contact in the persons of these three sufferers.

In the holy, spotless character of Jesus we have all that is highest, purest, best, in Heaven : in the repentance of one of the malefactors we have one seizing the final opportunity not granted to many on earth, of contrition, repentance, and acknowledgment of Christ as Lord, which means salvation ; whilst in the third we have, in his obstinacy, profanity and impiety, a striking example of the lost who are hardened in sin beyond the possibility of repentance.

Let us now proceed to consider the respective characters of the malefactors who suffered with our Lord. In the conduct of the penitent thief there is much that is extraordinary, deserving of our best attention. For some time he had joined the crowd and his fellow thief in reviling the Saviour, thus adding to His sufferings. It may be that in the course of his lawless wanderings he had heard the Saviour preaching, or healing, or feeding the multitude, or it may be by witnessing the sufferings of the One in the midst, no reviling words passed those lips, no bitterness, only prayer for His enemies, may have affected him. He may have had a Jewish father or Jewish mother from whose knees he may have heard something of this great Person. Whatever it is we do not know and are not allowed to speculate on since Scripture is silent, but we are privileged to see what conversion does, more quickly than a lightning flash. When God speaks there is blessing for the attentive ear and in less than a moment his destiny from hell to heaven and from a lawless abode to the Paradise above is his, together with a free pardon of his sin against God, although he still has to pay the penalty for his sin against society. But He "Who commanded the light to shine out of darkness" caused the light of truth to shine unto his mind to give him knowledge of himself and of the Son of God. In a moment He passed from death to life and changed his man from Adam to Christ. This is evidenced by his words. Confessing his own guilt he says in rebuke to the other thief, "And we indeed justly for we receive the due reward for our deeds, but this Man hath done nothing amiss." (Luke 23. 41.) *This is true repentance.* In the next verse he turns to the Saviour and says "Lord, remember me when Thou comest unto Thy Kingdom." *This is conversion.* In the following verse Jesus answers saying "Verily I say unto thee, to-day shalt thou be with me in Paradise." *This is eternal companionship* ; which only the sheep

72

know who hear the voice of the Good Shepherd.

And here we would say to those who think that they can go carelessly on with their sins like the thief and repent in the final hour of their life on earth, that it is given to none to know when his or her last hour shall be. Out of the millions who will tread the courts of heaven to only one has it been given the privilege " To-day shalt thou be with me in Paradise."

It would seem also from this incident that public confession of the name of the Lord on earth is necessary before we leave it for another world. One lesson, however, we may learn from this dying thief, and that is the complete illustration and vindication of the Saviour's words, " Him that cometh unto me I will in no wise cast out." Let the penitent, therefore, look up to Him, for His heart is full of tenderness although He now occupies the highest place in glory. His heart is as full of compassion now as when He expired on the Cross. In the repentant thief, therefore, we have on the one hand the greatest encouragement to come to Christ, and on the other the greatest possible warning not to defer this coming as another moment for the thief would have been too late !

Turning now to the impenitent malefactor, we observe that the treatment which our Lord received at his hands was truly remarkable. In Matthew's gospel (27. 44) :— " The thieves also that were crucified with Him cast the same in His teeth," whilst Luke tells us in chapter 23, verse 39, " One of the malefactors which were hanged railed on Him saying, ' if thou be the Christ save Thyself and us.' "

The conduct of this wretched man in reviling the Redeemer on the Cross illustrates for us not only the power of example but showing as a warning voice to us that, however near death a man may be, how far he can be from thinking seriously of the consequences of dying and of entering into the presence of a holy God. From the incidents before us we learn that a man may be occupied in his dying moments with that which does not at all concern him, and that so far from being in a state of mind suited to his dreadful situation he may be full of cursing and bitterness.

Does not this illustrate how all important it is not to defer the preparation of heart and mind for an eternal world ? Men (and preachers too) often speak of the penitent thief, and expect like him, in their last moments, to find repentance unto life. But how very rarely do they think on this remaining thief, who died unchanged ? The penitent thief receives grace and loses his sins at the Cross of his Saviour ; the impenitent thief abuses grace and so he dies with his sins upon him and will be raised again to answer for them at the great White Throne !

In our contemplation of the penitent thief, he mentions that Christ had a Kingdom, and no doubt the bitter cries and sneers of the elders of the people called his attention to the superscription over the Cross ; but his experience is that of every man who comes to Christ and speaks to Him from the heart, for whilst the thief looks on to a future moment for happiness the gracious accents of Christ fall upon his astonished ears, " *To-day* shalt thou be with me in Paradise," which in effect means :—" The happiness of being with Me shall not be deferred." And this is the experience of all who come to Christ. Paradise is mentioned three times only in Scripture : *For the repentant sinner* (Luke 23. 43), *For the saint who serves* (2 Corinthians 12. 4), *For the overcomer who endures* (Revelation 2. 7). Every believer in Christ (1) commences as a repentant sinner, (2) continues as a serving saint (for God changes his name from sinner to saint), and (3) is looked at as an overcomer in God's eye. Whether he believes or not is another matter, for we get such words as " Who is he that overcometh the world but he who believes that Jesus is the Son of God " (1 John 5. 5), and the victory in the previous verse we are told which overcomes the world is " our faith." What joy awaits the believer in the coming world of glory for the word is " To-day with Me." Paradise without the company of the Saviour would lose its sweetness.

To conclude :—the contemplation of the malefactors crucified (by the world's derision as the suffering Saviour's guard of honour) in that unspeakable moment of all moments, teach us only too plainly that the world is divided into two classes, saved and unsaved. It is not a little remarkable that the suffering Saviour enters the unseen world first, that by His death He might prepare a place for the repentant thief, and in fact when the thief is launched out of time into eternity by the breaking of his legs, the Son of God was there to welcome and receive him into Paradise.

We have remarked earlier not only of the coming to Christ but of the enjoyment of it. Enjoyment is based on present company with Christ, for the experience of the apostle Paul was expressed in language as seen in the first chapter of his letter to the Philippians, stating, "For me to live is Christ, and to die is gain, but if I live in the flesh this is the fruit of my labour" (that is, Christ is my life), yet what I shall choose I wot not for I am in a strait betwixt two, having a desire to depart and be with Christ, which is far better. (Philippians 1. 21-23.)

The dying thief beheld that Lamb,
 Expiring by His side,
And proved the value of the Name,
 Of Jesus crucified.
His soul by virtue of the Blood
 To Paradise received,
Redemption's earliest trophy stood,
 From sin and death retrieved.

CHAPTER VII.

SIMON PETER WHO DENIED THE SAVIOUR.

" But he began to curse and swear saying I know not this Man of whom ye speak."—Mark 14. 71.

THE infamous conduct of one of the disciples of our Lord, Judas, and his betrayal of his Master, has already been considered by us, and now we propose to contemplate the great denial of one who whilst a genuine disciple trusted to the arm of flesh and thereby afforded for all time a lesson to every follower of the Lord Jesus Christ :—Of the folly of trusting to natural ardour instead of leaning on the arm of Christ alone. The lesson afforded us in our consideration of Judas is deeply instructive together with its being a fearful spectacle of the slippery descent of sin.

But in Peter's case it is calculated to give us also many tears as it did to that of Peter, lest we too trust in the arm of flesh and miss this most important lesson of counting on Christ alone.

Peter's fall was aggravated by the repeated warnings which he received. First he tells the Saviour in the Passion Week that he loved Him so much that if all the other disciples denied Him he would remain steadfast. Gently and kindly the Saviour tells him that he was the subject of His prayers, " I have prayed for thee," for Satan desired to sift him as wheat.

Let us notice in order the warnings that he received. First, Judas had just left the Upper Room in which the last Passover was celebrated, and the Son of Man had spoken to the remaining eleven after his departure and exhorted them to mutual love. Simon Peter then said, " Lord, whither goeth Thou ? " And the Saviour answered, " Where I go, you cannot follow now, but you shall do so after." When Peter said in much affection, " Lord, why cannot I follow Thee now, I will lay down my life for Thee ? " Jesus answered, " Wilt thou lay down thy life for my sake ? Verily, verily I say unto thee, the cock doth not crow till thou hast denied me thrice." (John 13. 36-38.)

The second warning is a little later on in the same room. Some of the disciples were talking together as to who would be accounted the greatest in the Kingdom. A little selfishly they had forgotten the One in whose presence they were, and of how His tender heart must have been torn by their demeanour. Graciously the Blessed Saviour tells them, " Ye are they which have continued with me in my temptations," and like His servant Elisha in an earlier day, He thus throws a handful of meal (typical of Christ) into the pot where there was poison working, and thus ended the strife. It would seem that immediately Simon Peter was implicated as a prime mover, for He says to him, " Behold, Satan has desired to have you that he may sift you as wheat, but I have prayed for thee that thy faith fail not ; and when thou art converted, strengthen thy brethren." (Luke 22. 24-32.)

On the third occasion of warning, on the way from the upper room to the Mount of Olives and thence to Gethsemane, our Lord still conversed with them and foretold their desertion of Him that night. The mind of impulsive but affectionate Peter was filled with the circumstances of the last Supper. It was not given to him to record the Lord's prayer ; this was the privilege afforded to John alone in the 17th chapter of John's Gospel. But they had sung the hymns associated with the Last Supper. They had therefore sung together with Jesus in their midst Psalms 116, 117 and 118, and no doubt Peter was very moved at the pause which followed verse 8 of the 118th Psalm, which is the exact centre of the Bible itself, " It is better to trust in the Lord than to put confidence in princes," and how affecting to them all, when a little lower down we have those words which were sung not only by them as the choir, but the Son of God, Who was the Choir Master Himself, " God is Jehovah who has shewed us light bind the sacrifice with cords even to the horns of the altar." Then the third warning is given to Peter. " Thus saith Jesus unto them, all ye shall be offended because of me this night ; for it is written, I will smite the shepherd and the sheep of the flock shall be scattered abroad. But after I am risen again I will go before you unto Galilee." Peter answered and said unto Him, " Though all men shall be offended because of Thee yet will I never be offended." Jesus said unto him, " Verily I say unto thee that before the cock crow thou shalt deny me thrice." Peter said unto Him, " Though I would die for Thee yet I will not deny Thee." Likewise also said all the disciples. (Matt. 26. 30-35.)

We thus see that he was warned three times by our Lord and there was no excuse for him. If those warnings had been given three years before or even twelve months before they might reasonably be forgotten by Peter, but it was less than twelve hours afterwards, actually in the same night when the offence was committed, of denying his Master. In between the period of warnings and that of committal there was the history

F

of the Garden and all its associations, and here Peter, we are told, was fast asleep when he was particularly requested by his Master to watch with Him at least one hour. We thus assume that ignorance of what the flesh can do, coupled with lack of power, must be a fatal circumstance for any Christian, especially as in the last closing words of the ministry of Christ we have Him saying, " Watch and pray, and what I say unto you I say unto all, watch."

Passing then from Gethsemane and its sorrow and Peter's ardour and courage in protecting his Master by using the sword which caused the last public act of the Saviour to be that of healing (for He covered His servant's serious blunder by healing the right ear of the High Priest's servant (Luke 22. 50-51), we will deal with the incidents surrounding the three denials.

First Denial :—First we find that when our Lord surrendered Himself to the soldiers the eleven forsook Him and fled, and two of them, when they found they were not pursued turned back to follow the Lord afar off ; John was one, the other was Peter. John apparently was acquainted with the High Priest, and speaking to the portress, a young woman who kept the door, he takes Peter in along with him. And now the test comes, for out in the courtyard it was early morning and intensely cold, for the winter spells still hung over Jerusalem. The fire has been kindled and the civil soldiers gather round.

Peter, who was prayerless and sleeping in the Garden, is attracted by the warmth of the world's fire, and the young maid belonging to the staff of the High Priest sees him and challenges him with the words : " And thou also wast with Jesus of Nazareth," but he denies this and says, " I know not neither understand what thou sayest." And when he went out into the porch, the first rays of early morning sun caused the cock to crow. This was the first denial.

Second Denial :—The examination of the sinless Saviour continues and the High Priest is asking Him concerning His disciples and His doctrine, and Peter hearing this fears on account of his activity in the Garden when he smote the servant of the High Priest and dreading detection he goes to the porch probably intending to flee, and the one who said, " I will go with Thee to prison and to death " is once again tested and once again fails. Another maid belonging to the staff of the High Priest looks at him earnestly and says to those who stood by, " This is one of them," and again he denies, but to give emphasis to his denial he adds an oath which makes his denial more solemn still.

Alas, there is nothing to choose now between him and the poor worldling. It is a case of bad, leading to worse ! And Peter goes lower down in the scale missing this glorious opportunity of confessing for his Saviour.

Third Denial :—Things have now settled down a little, but it is still cold in the porch and there is everything there to render his situation most uncomfortable. The Saviour is questioned again respecting His disciples and these have led to no disclosures, so faithful is the Saviour to His followers, so Peter returns again to the hall and covers himself as well as possible and sits by the fire quietly for the space of one hour. It is no doubt affection for his Master which brings him back again ; conscience stirs in his breast, and although he has just denied Him he exposes himself again to danger, to hear and to see what the position will be in regard to his Master and Lord. But his very effort to escape notice calls attention to him, and the kinsman of Malchus whose ear   had cut off states that he saw him in the Garden when Jesus was apprehended, and when he is questioned again, his accent as being that of a Galilean betrays him as such. And now for Peter the danger increases and he loses his calm which every disciple should possess and retain, and also to prove that he did not know Him he began to curse and to swear, saying " I know not this man of whom ye speak." How dreadful this is, for he is now acting like a conscience-less person who has no fear of God before his eyes, if we may judge from his language. It is not the language of heaven or even of earth but of hell itself !

This last denial was done in the very presence of the Saviour, for we read that the cock crew again, " And the Lord turned and looked upon Peter, and Peter remembered the word of the Lord how He said unto him, Before the cock crow thou shalt deny me thrice. And Peter went out and wept bitterly."

What a moment this would have been for Peter to have stood firm ; for the position was this, his Master had been apprehended, the disciples had all fled, one of them had even betrayed his Lord, Jesus was in the hands of sinners who thirsted for His blood, danger and death surrounded the Saviour as dark-ness surrounded the scene, but instead of protecting the One who had been so kind to him, he uses every effort to escape the snare by which he was beset.

What may we learn from the case of

Peter ? We learn the nature of true repentance which leads to life. Judas was filled with remorse, the remorse of a world which has a sting but does not lift one above the condition of self-despair, and leads to suicide. But in the case of Peter, who was no more sincere than that of Judas, we have the fruits which accompany salvation.

If our Blessed Lord had rescued himself from His enemies, Judas, the one who betrayed Him, would have felt no sense of shame or sorrow and would have looked upon his thirty pieces of silver with awful satisfaction. With him it was coveteousness which led to idolatry that caused him to lose his soul and life. But with Peter it was different; he was now brought face to face with the offence in itself as a ruling principle, and feeling that he had sinned against truth and conscience he knew he had wronged his own soul, which filled him with sorrow and shame, and thinking thereon, he wept bitterly. When his Master looked upon him, it was not only the effect of the look which broke him down, bringing home to him the thought of his own shame, but no doubt he read underneath that look, this fact that if his Redeemer had spoken reminding him of his trespass and promise, it would have betrayed his disciple, and this would have been entirely contrary to the service of divine love.

It is not a little significant that when Peter followed afar off his natural characteristics came to the front. In his youth as a fisherman, he was no doubt accustomed to swearing, for it must be remembered that Peter had a very hot temper naturally, as may be indicated by his wanting to be always in the forefront. We know many persons who, when they are in company at all, have never learned the art of listening, but must be speaking all the time ; such persons we have discovered to be impulsive, self-willed and certainly not under the control of Heaven, or accustomed to the presence of the Lord.

Peter thought that long contact with Christ for three years had caused this to be dead and buried long since, but applying it to ourselves as confessed disciples of Christ, if we are not walking in the sense of the Lord's presence constantly and are content to follow afar off, we shall never get rid of what is peculiar to us naturally, and old habits will crush, if not blot out, the workings of the new life.

There is a very happy finish to Peter's grievous fall which we will now consider in conclusion. Although Peter had behaved so shamefully, and there is not much difference between his sin and that of Judas, underneath there was his genuine love for his Master and Lord, and Christ knew it as He knows all our hearts. The first thing, therefore, that the risen Lord does is to appear to Peter before He appears to the twelve as recorded in 1 Corinthians 15. 5. This was no doubt a special service rendered in order to assure Peter that God had forgiven him for slighting His Son, and so Peter was the first disciple to receive blessing.

However, there was much more to be done, for if we as believers have sinned against light and love (and confessedly it is true of us all), "if any man sin we have an advocate with the Father, Jesus Christ the righteous," to bring us back to communion. Such are our hearts that we are afraid to return lest we break down again so that we may say that the sin is more rapid in point of time than restoration, and of course this is as it should be.

Reverting back to Peter, we find that it was necessary not only to be privately restored but publicly so to the confidence of his fellow brethren, and so the risen Son of God wastes no time in bringing about this desired result. Which brings us to the 21st Chapter of the Gospel according to John which is full of Jesus and Peter. Here we may remark that right through the protective ministry of Christ for three and a half wonderful years the disciples never lacked anything as He Himself challenges them at the end of that ministry. But now they are left to their own resources, and Peter tells them that he is going fishing to provide for the needs of the body ; but on this occasion the Lord supplies the need with this difference to that of the first occasion (see 5th chapter of Luke's Gospel, verse 6), that here the net does not break since in resurrection nothing can break down. But the great service of the Saviour now is to consider and satisfy their spiritual needs, and so Peter is publicly restored. Three times he had broken down and three times the whole work must be gone into that the restoration might be completed and permanent until he is forced to say " Thou knowest all things, Thou knowest I have affection for Thee."

> But gracious Lord when we reflect
> How apt to turn the eye from Thee,
> Forget Thee, too, with sad neglect,
> And listen to the enemy,
> And yet to find Thee still the same—
> 'Tis this that humbles us with shame.
>
> Astonished at Thy feet we fall,
> Thy love exceeds our highest thought ;
> Henceforth be Thou our all-in-all,
> Thou who our souls with Blood hast bought
> May we henceforth more faithful prove,
> And ne'er forget Thy ceaseless love.

CHAPTER VIII.

THE DISCIPLES WHO DESERTED THE SAVIOUR.

"And they all forsook Him and fled."
—Mark 14. 50.

THIS short sentence in the records of holy Scripture is perhaps one of the most painful ever given. The Blessed Saviour had endured a whole public life of shameful opposition from the religious leaders, but now He was to experience a still further trial.

Those men who were His companions sharing His lot were now to turn tail in the very hour of His deep need. We have to turn to the Psalms in order to understand His emotions on this dire occasion where we read such touching words as " Looking for comforters and found none (Psalm 69). (Psalm 18 is the Gethsemane Psalm ; Psalm 69 is the Psalm of Desertion ; Psalm 22 is the Psalm of Atoning ; Psalm 77 is the Psalm of Doom echoed by those in hell through refusing Christ. Verse 7 : " Cast off for ever," " favourable no more " ; verse 8 :

" mercy clean gone for ever." " promise fail for evermore " ; verse 9 : " forgotten to be gracious," " in anger shut up His tender mercies." What a dreadful echo !) We know indeed that their love had not given way to enmity, neither was there any alteration in their sentiments and feelings for their Master and Lord ; they fully believed in His Messiahship but they had yet to learn the nature and character of the Kingdom which He had come to establish.

Alas, ambition, we find, played a very large part in their thoughts, as shown in the last Passover Supper. These few simple, illiterate fishermen saw themselves chief ministers of the greatest empire in the world, and this, taking possession of their minds, excluded everything else. Becoming an obsession with them, they found no room for receiving their Lord's plain unvarnished statements respecting His sufferings and death.

Time and again, especially during the last year of His ministry amongst them, He had inculcated the necessity of such death as the way to the Throne of Glory, and if He was to have companions to share that Throne, His co-sharers must know that only through tribulation could we enter the Kingdom.

The dismay of Judas when he saw the Man of Sorrows allowing Himself to be led away by the band of enemies on that all memorable night of base betrayal, was shared by the apostles themselves—their false notions, alas, contributed to render them an easy prey to the enemy. What an object lesson for us to rightly divide the Word of Truth lest we hinder the work of God instead of being His co-workers. All this but added to the suffering of our Blessed Lord.

Adorable Saviour and Lord; His must be the experience of the wormwood and the gall fully partaken of that we might be free! Then we should consider the fact that the desertion of the disciples came as an added aggravation to the sufferings of our Lord. It should not be forgotten in considering the Blessed Person of the Christ—very God and very Man—that he was made in all points like His brethren.

He had all the affections and feelings of human nature just as we have, sin apart. The great difference between us is that whilst in us they are constantly liable to perversion and abuse, in Him their exercise was always healthy and legitimate. So that whilst it may be true that when we are " let down," as we say, by others from whom we have expected different treatment and our grief at such betrayal of our love and confidence is deep-seated and real, how very much more accentuated to the gentle holy mind of the Lord Jesus to receive such unfaithfulness, unkindness, desertion, especially at the moment of His trouble. He had a right to expect fidelity from His friends, but, alas, one of them had betrayed Him—another was shortly to deny Him—and in this His extremity they all forsook Him and fled ! Alas, what is man ?

They had been privileged witnesses of His acts of power, of healing, of raising from the dead, giving sight to the blind, feeding a hungry multitude. Then at the close He says (John 16. 32) " Behold the hour cometh, yea, is now come, that ye shall be scattered every man to his own, and shall leave me alone ; and yet I am not alone because the Father is with me." That He felt to the full this tragic desertion is shown in the prophetic writings such as Psalm 69. 20 : " Reproach hath broken my heart : and I am full of heaviness : and I looked for some to take pity, but there was none : and for comforters, but I found none."

Then He employed the feelings of David on the occasion of the treason of Ahithophel, and David's sorrow at the wrongdoing of his favourite son Absalom brought about through the mistakes of David. Jesus had no mistakes to recall. Their desertion then was a cup of bitterness drunk to the full by Christ. We repeat, He had a right to calculate on the fidelity of His friends—those whom He had named and commissioned as His apostles—but alas, such is man :—the sermon on the Mount uttered three years before with its consideration for others had by this time been forgotten by them.

The fact that those who had pursued Him for His life were near, had only a secondary place before His own. How lonely had been the earthly pathway of this Man of Sorrows. In His acquaintanceship with grief He was a lonely holy Stranger to His chosen loved ones. Three from amongst them had been favoured with witnessing His glory on the Mount of Transfiguration, which had so profoundly affected one of them that when he was an old man in years and service he writes of it on the threshold of eternity just before his martyrdom, " This is my beloved Son in whom I am well pleased, and this voice which came from Heaven we heard when we were with Him on the holy mount." (2 Peter 1. 17-18.)

Then towards the close of His earthly ministry the disciples had viewed with joy the acclamations of the young children welcoming Him to Jerusalem as the rightful King and Ruler, and the thrill of the occasion had led their thoughts and aspirations to that day which surely, say they, must be almost present. But the fact was, He must die before this could be accomplished according to His Father's Counsels, and now terrified they had succumbed to the first shock of the enemy's thrust and of Christ's apparent defeat, for He says " This is your hour and the power of darkness."

The great thing they had overlooked was the dignity of the Man of Sorrows on this occasion. They had just witnessed one from among them having betrayed Him, and the shock of this, instead of welding them together, had bewildered them, and caused them to flee as cowards, and indeed as wicked men, for it says, " The wicked flee when no man pursueth." And what of the Saviour ? His tender shepherd heart had gone out protectively towards them and He says, " If ye seek me let these go their way."

Like the type seen in David, who before he meets Goliath on behalf of Israel, he leaves his father's sheep in the hands of a keeper, so Christ the great eternal Lover has already handed over His loved sheep to His Father in His marvellous prayer (John 17).

Did these things not speak to them ?

Undoubtedly any one of the angels in heaven deeply concerned now and watching with eager interest would gladly have forfeited future glory to have been permitted to protect this One ; but no, He must tread the winepress Himself, *alone* !

These prayerless and therefore unprepared disciples were of no service to the Christ of God in His deep need, and so it has ever been. To be prayerless is to be unprepared. It may be objected that they were unconverted since they had not yet the Spirit, but surely His call looked on to the Cross and its accomplishment, and the gift of the Spirit was afterwards given to finally secure them for God. Afterwards, indeed, they were privileged to witness for Him by martyrdom according to Church history, but one cannot but be touched by His sorrow as seen in Psalm 69. 20, already quoted !

We turn away with glad relief to the faithful love of the Lord Jesus in that desertion hour ; many waters could not quench His love. All the ingratitude of man could not affect its even flow ; and all the powers of darkness could not destroy it. Blessed Redeemer and Lover. " Having loved His own which were in the world, He loved them to the end."

It may well be that the unfaithfulness of the apostles was permitted that Jesus might taste of every ingredient mingled in the cup of woe, and that being tempted in all points like unto His brethren He might be able to succour and sympathise with them in their temptations. We may well exclaim " O love that will not let me go." It has been said by someone, " When He was doing all for man that infinite love could do for them, they hated Him or deserted Him. When He was dying for the world, the world persecuted Him. When He was giving His life for His friends, His friends " forsook Him and fled."

What a lesson of encouragement this has been to the poor unhappy backslider in all ages, for notwithstanding all their desertion, Jesus did not disown them ; for after His resurrection having atoned for their sins on the Cross of shame, He sent to them by the faithful women, messages of tenderness and love. " Go to My brethren and say unto them, I ascend unto My Father and your Father ; to my God and your God " (John 20. 17) was His message through Mary Magdalene. And also through the other women, " Go tell my brethren that I go into Galilee and there shall they see me " (Matthew 28. 10).

G

So we may say that the defection of the disciples only brought out more fully His faithfulness. Precious Saviour!

We wait for Thee, content to share,
  In patience, days of trial;
So meekly Thou the Cross didst bear,
  Our sin, reproach, denial.
How should not we receive with Thee
  The cup of shame and sorrow,
  Until the promised morrow?

We wait for Thee, for Thou e'en here
  Hast won our heart's affection,
In spirit still we find Thee near,
  Our solace and protection.
In cloudless light and glory bright,
  We soon with joy shall greet Thee,
  And in the air shall meet Thee.

CHAPTER IX.

THE WOMEN WHO MINISTERED TO THE SAVIOUR.

" And certain women . . . . ministered to Him
of their substance."

—Luke 8. 2-3.

DURING the last closing scenes of the Saviour's
sojourn on earth and before the darkening
clouds were gathering about His Blessed
Person, it is very refreshing to read of the
women who cared for Him so devotedly,
and one can understand the joy it gave the
angels immediately after the resurrection
of our Lord (yea on the very morning) to
utter words of comfort to them, especially
as we earlier read in the sacred pages of
inspired truth that they were near the Cross
when the others had fled, remaining there
until the last, and they were afterwards first
at the tomb. All honour, devoted women,
for your constancy and strength of affection.
It may be said that they were Galilean
women, but they certainly could be designated
" holy " women !

Of one, indeed, the Saviour speaks when

He says, " But wisdom is justified of all her children," for the poor sinful woman of Luke 7 had confessed her sin in the presence of the holy Son of God—the personification of wisdom and He had justified her publicly.

Then another appreciates His holy footsteps and expends her all upon Him, and we read " The house was *filled* with the odour of the ointment."

A third one just weeps at the sepulchre and sobs out her sorrows to the angels : " They have taken away *my* Lord."

All these lighten the dark background of what the Blessed Man of Sorrows endured during His gracious serving ministry to ungrateful beings, and so often our thoughts as we think in retrospection upon the sad defection of His own. These women were indeed amongst the excellent of the earth, and their conduct is beyond praise or computation of worth. They were the subjects of a holy, ardent, reverent affection for One whom they justly regarded as the living representation of wisdom, truth, gentleness, and goodness.

They had for many years followed Him in His many journeys of kindness and lowly service through the cities and villages of Palestine. Very gladly had they ministered to Him of their substance, and it afforded them the deepest joy and gratification of heart.

We cannot but think that they laboured in every possible way to promote His comfort, to alleviate His sufferings, to lessen His toils as unweariedly He pursued His lonely way from the manger to the Cross. It will never be forgotten by God and a coming day will fully declare this tender service of selfless devotedness.

In this present day when women are so much in evidence in business, politics, religious activity, and in social service, how very refreshing to think of these devoted ones quietly working in the background unobtrusively and quietly, this one sentence at the head of our chapter epitomising true worth as against the sham service of so many who make a great noise with nothing at the end thereof.

We are not told who wove the seamless garment which Jesus wore, but we know that love had done this. And how touching to learn that the blessed Redeemer in His goodness and gentleness without question accepted all these tokens of love and valued them as proofs and expressions of the ardent attachment from which they proceeded. And how affecting to think that this affection of theirs remained constant through all circumstances, and that the change in the circumstances of the Saviour changed them not one iota.

We know that these dear devoted women were not with Him on the night of betrayal, else that Scripture would never have been true, " They all forsook Him and fled."

How, indeed, this characteristic is true of women of every age. Nothing can change them when love is there. Her husband is erring, or her son becomes prodigal, and she is incapable of seeing any deterioration of character in the object of her love. She thinks through her heart in contrast to the man who thinks through his mind. He is without doubt right in his reasoning faculties, but his sacrifice, if any, is cold and repelling.

But the wife or the mother—ah, how true then that " Love covers a multitude of sins." Is he in danger, she prays ; in peril, she promptly acts.

History itself is brilliantly lit up with the glorious services of selfless devoted women. So with these ministering women following the Man of Sorrows. Peter may shrink before a maid and tremblingly say " I know Him not "—but they tremble at no power ; the whole world shall know that they are His. So they remained around the Cross the six hours the Redeemer suffers there.

They are unmoved at the frenzied yells of the " Bulls of Bashan," the threats and derision of the wicked priests, the swords and staves of the soldiers. Nothing can terrify them or drive them away from the One they love. Thus they remain when the multitude have dispersed, and they eagerly note the place where He is buried. Then early on the resurrection day they are first at the grave.

Neither cold, nor darkness, nor Roman guard can alter them or affect their constant and quiet loyalty. The eleven indeed said " We will die with Thee, but we will not deny Thee." Alas, they in the hour of testing proved untrue.

The holy women said nothing, but they did the right thing at the right moment. Like Martha and Mary in their hour of grief, these women would equally have said " I believe that Thou art the Christ, the Son of God, which should have come into the world."

Their faith and trust were based on a just appreciation as well as a clear perception of true moral worth. There may have been many difficulties concerning the subject of the Messiahship of the Lord Jesus, but these they would leave others to solve ; theirs was the joy of witnessing simply, loyally and unquestionably that " Jesus was the Son of God and that believing they would have life through His name."

How very refreshing to the Saviour of sinners during His great service of love to find such clinging loving hearts to eternal goodness as expressed in Him. This loyalty produced in itself a very heavenly fruit in that they were ready to credit at once the testimony of the glorious beings whom they saw at the open grave. It was there that the angels told them that their Lord had risen. The testimony in Matthew 28. 5-8 is exquisitely given :—" I know that ye seek Jesus which was crucified. He is not here : for He is risen, as He said. Come see the place where the Lord lay. And go quickly and tell His disciples that He is risen from the dead ; and behold, He goeth before you into Galilee : there ye shall see Him : lo, I have told you And they departed quickly from the sepulchre with fear and great joy ; and did *run* to bring the disciples word." We bring in the whole of the inspired word because the emphasis is on the fact that they *ran* in order to give the glad news.

Alas, we are told " their words seemed to them as idle tales : they believed them not," for desertion and unbelief are twin sisters.

The renewed mind when not under the control of the Spirit of God is cold and calculating, but where the affections are at work understanding must take a second place. And no doubt it was a reward of their fidelity and affection that they were privileged to be the first informed of their Lord's resurrection.

It is noteworthy that these visions of angels did not appear at all to the brethren, and our Lord Himself appeared twice to the women before He appeared to the disciples—apart perhaps from Peter. How very true is the word " Them that honour me I will honour."

Let our sisters learn the greatest possible comfort and encouragement from the dear devoted women and their service to their Lord in the moments of His great need, and may we all as professed followers of His with shame take the lowest place at our Saviour's feet to Whom be praise and glory.

Lord we are Thine : bought by Thy blood,
  Once the poor guilty slaves of sin,
But Thou redeemest us to God,
  And made'st Thy spirit dwell within ;
Thou hast our sinful wanderings borne
  With love and patience all divine :
As brands then from the burning torn,
  We own that we are wholly Thine.

THE STORY OF THE CROSS.

Lord we are Thine, Thy claims we own,
  Ourselves to Thee we'd wholly give ;
Reign Thou within our hearts alone
  And let us to Thy glory live :
Here let us each Thy mind display,
  In all Thy gracious image shine,
And haste that long expected day
  When Thou shalt own that we are Thine.

CHAPTER X.

The Disciple Who Remained With The Saviour.

"Now there was leaning on Jesus' bosom one of His disciples whom Jesus loved."
—John 13. 23.

WE have considered several characteristics of those privileged persons who spoke to the Saviour during His public ministry on earth up to the close of that service, and have viewed with alarm, grief and sorrow, the activities of Judas, Peter and the remaining disciples in their sad indifference to His heart's longings, and with pleasure we have turned aside to note the loyalty of the true-hearted women who cared for Him.

With great pleasure we would now examine the conduct of the disciple whom Jesus loved (John the beloved apostle).

Millions of years yet to come, many will re-live those thrilling scenes of our beloved Lord's earthly sojourn, and the glorified in heaven—those who came to Christ during His present rejection as guilty sinners, and found eternal life through thus coming—

will dwell particularly upon the last supper and its touching surroundings, which we will now carefully consider as John of our chapter has given the fullest account.

Most likely this is because those scenes and circumstances affected his mind most profoundly and so he has for our instruction and comfort left them on record. Here we find him leaning on the bosom of Jesus with great favour and honour. And just as it seemed most natural for Judas to be the treasurer without question, so we see John in this favoured place, and the question naturally arises : Why is he so distinguished ? He was generally supposed to be of the same age as our Lord, and it may be granted that, everything else being equal, persons of the same age are much more likely to enter into each other's feelings and sentiments, and, indeed, apart from one small incident when Jesus had to administer the rebuke " Forbid him not . . . for he that is not against us is for us " (Mark 9. 38-40), John appeared to enter more fully into His thoughts than the others. Then the natural disposition of our Beloved Redeemer was that of meekness, gentleness, tenderness to others and their need ; which appears to be that of John also, reading between the lines of his written ministry. His was a nature peculiarly mild and loving, and where he rebukes severely it was only because of love's necessity, and indeed in meriting the Lord's rebuke as above mentioned it would appear that the unfairness of the one casting out demons in his Master's name lay in the fact that he was declining to associate himself with the rest of the disciples, which hurt John so much.

It was this love for his Master which caused him to indignantly request the Lord to cause that fire should come down from heaven to consume the Samaritans because they would not receive Him on His journey to Jerusalem.

Such was John the beloved disciple, and we may gather how the Saviour in glory to-day loves the gentleness, meekness, forbearance of His own, causing them to merit this place of favour and privilege, once accorded on earth to John. It is John who has favoured God's people with the prayer of the Son to His Father in which those people find what a marvellous place they have in the eternal affections of the Son. (John 17.)

John had followed the movements of Christ right from the moment of his being called to follow Him, and had watched His days of exertion on behalf of the needy, then His retirement at night in prayer, and had noted the more laborious and active the day, the more watchful and prayerful the succeeding night of the Saviour. And following to Gethsemane on the last night— the night of betrayal, He retires with the eleven to the Mount of Olives :—eight of them are left at the wicket gate of a certain garden, probably belonging to one of His friends to which He often went for retirement and devotion. The remaining three, of whom John was one, were taken with Him in this garden, and to these He does not conceal His deep feelings, and with a full heart He begs their sympathy and watchfulness.

He says, " My soul is exceeding sorrowful even unto death ; sit ye here, while I go and pray yonder. (Matt. 26. 36.)

Did they watch and pray ? Alas, no ; numbed with the early spring night cold, heavy with grief and sorrow, they wrapped their cloaks around them and fell asleep, whilst their Master and Lord was praying in an agony, as we read, " His sweat was as it were great drops of blood falling down to the ground." No earthly eye beholds this sorrow ; it is left for the holy Spirit of God to pen the words that we might watch and pray lest we might enter into temptation.

His chief friends whom He had honoured as on other occasions such as on the Mount of Transfiguration, instead of comforting Him were sleeping, and of that trio of favoured of all persons John was one. Waking them up, the Eternal Lover gently reproves them with : " What, could ye not watch with me one hour." A second time this happens and then a third. And now His agony becomes deeper and more mysterious ; His heart is overwhelmed within Him ; His soul sinks into deep waters, where there is no standing ; and nature sinks beneath the awful load of this Gethsemane sorrow. But He is heard, thank God :—Psalm 18 (the Gethsemane Psalm where He is heard because of His piety) must precede Psalm 22 (Calvary and its forsaking because of sin's awful load ; on behalf of the poor sinful man He the sinless, spotless, stainless Victim must suffer).

Asleep through it all, John, bewildered and fearful at the band of armed ruffians, sees the Redeemer voluntarily yielding Himself to His enemies, and with the rest of the disciples forsakes Him, and flees, leaving Him alone. Well indeed was it for John and for us that our Beloved Saviour's heart is filled with tenderness and forgiveness and that our God multiplies pardon through the work of the Cross.

After the first shock and terror has passed John resumes his tranquility of mind and follows at a distance his Master, with Peter as a companion, and with inward apprehensions they wait outside whilst Jesus is detained in the palace of Annas. Following the band which reforms outside with Jesus in the midst they pursue their way to the palace of Caiaphas, where as John was known he enters and brings in Peter through his influence. This is the place where Peter denies his Lord.

Alas, if only Peter had thought over those words " this man also was with Him " he would have considered that John was known there as His follower, and his heart would have been strengthened to confess Him in the hour of His great need of friendship !

From this time onward John remains the close friend of his Master and steadfastly adheres to Him, manifested the deepest sympathy and at the Cross was ready to discharge whatever service his Master called for, and so, in His closing earthly hours, with those hands once caressing little children now outstretched on the Cross of shame to embrace with love and forgiveness a guilty world, the thrice worthy Saviour finds some consolation amidst His deepest injuries and His heaviest woes, and when heaven itself was about to forsake Him because of the necessity of a complete satisfaction of His vicarious substitutionary sufferings. We stay to consider John at the Cross. What a day that must have been in Jerusalem.

Firstly, immense multitudes were there to celebrate the Passover. (It has been computed that there were over two million people thronging its streets on this occasion.) It was the eve of a double Sabbath (the ordinary weekly one and the paschal Sabbath), and as before mentioned the probable year of Jubilee.

Then the public mind had been greatly agitated by the miracles, ministry, and claims of the Lord Jesus as Messiah, and they heard that He had been arrested, condemned at both the ecclesiastical and civil tribunals, publicly refused by the nation, and now crucified between two robbers. Multitudes must have followed Him through the gate of Jerusalem to Calvary a mile away, and gazed upon Him on the Cross, and as we go with them we do not see Peter and the rest of the men disciples, but we do see John standing near the Cross sharing His reproach.

John takes the arm of the widowed and bereaved mother of Jesus, for now " a sword must pierce her own soul," and Jesus observes them there and addressing them says, " Woman, behold thy Son : then

113

H

saith He to His disciple, Behold thy mother.
And from that hour that disciple took her
unto his own home." (John 19. 26-27.)

Thus amidst the execrations of the rulers
and priests and people the Son of God, who
came from heaven's glory to this humiliating
Cross of shame in order to become the Saviour
of the World, He who was and is the sovereign
Judge and Creator of the Universe, enters
upon the second phase of his distress with the
one solitary consolation of having committed
to the disciple whom He loved the secret
of His earthly parentage.

Adam had no father or mother; we
necessarily have both earthly father and
mother; the Blessed Saviour had an earthly
mother but no earthly father; God was His
Father.

John now leads his new mother away;
it is the end of the first three hours on the
Cross, and before the actual forsaking by
God, and our next consideration of John
must be at the grave of Jesus.

In passing we may call attention to a
remarkable circumstance. The Saviour had
many times in His closing ministry talked
freely of His sufferings, death and resurrection from the dead on the third day, but
strange to say they never seem to have entertained it in their minds, and even when He

was reported risen with the tomb empty and hearing the testimony of the angels they did not believe : yet the enemies of our Lord had, in anticipation of the third day taken every precaution to prevent His resurrection. It would appear that Satan believed and knew in some mysterious way that everything would depend on keeping the Blessed Lord in the darkness of the grave. In fact, Christianity owes its triumph to resurrection, as we know by blessed experience.

But although the disciples were far from anticipating His resurrection, the women were early at the tomb on the morning of the third day—not indeed to welcome the Risen Saviour and Lord, but to render the last touching office of affection to His sacred remains. With surprise and much fear they found the stone rolled away, their fear being accentuated by the thought that His enemies had treated His body with further shame. But Mary Magdalene, probably the youngest, certainly the most ardent in her love, runs to tell Peter and John of the extraordinary occurrence (it was afterwards when she had the blessed experience of speaking to the Lord personally).

And now John, in youthful agility, outruns Peter, and, we read, " he saw and believed " (John 20. 8). In Luke's record we read that Peter departed wondering, but John believed the women and was the first one to be blessed, and the only one of the disciples to believe the resurrection of their Lord simply from an inspection of the grave. One wonders if this confirmed something the Saviour had said to him privately during the holy hours of their communion.

John thus was calm and happy in the conviction that his beloved Lord was risen, and that He had triumphed over His enemies.

Afterwards it was given to John to unfold the wondrous unveilings of future glory and subsequent overthrow of evil—to see his Master acknowledged as King of kings and Lord of lords in the beautiful foreshadowing in the Book of Revelation, and finally to write about the eternal state when God shall dwell with men in a new heaven and new earth, where sin cannot intrude and life and righteousness shall be the alone principles of activity and movement.

Fairer than all the earthborn race,
Perfect in comeliness Thou art ;
Replenished are Thy lips with grace,
And full of love Thy tender heart.
God ever blest ! we bow the knee,
And own all fullness dwells in Thee.

THE STORY OF THE CROSS.

Be Thou the object, bright and fair,
   To fill and satisfy the heart ;
Our hope to meet Thee in the air,
   And nevermore from Thee to part :
That we may undistracted be
To follow, serve and wait for Thee.

CHAPTER XI.

THE TWO COUNCILLORS WHO BURIED THE SAVIOUR.

" And after this Joseph of Arimathaea, being a disciple of Jesus . . . . also Nicodemus . . . . then took they the body of Jesus."
—John 19. 38-40.

THE conduct of Joseph and Nicodemus on the occasion of our Lord's burial has brought out the grateful thanks of God's redeemed, and in that fact that our Lord was buried by these two we have the accomplishment of the prediction of Scripture as well as the undeniable proof of His resurrection. Isaiah 53 tells us among other precious things that " He made His grave with the wicked, but He was with the rich in His death."

Such was man's appointment, but the atoning work was now over, and God intervened by loving care and tender hands to render this last office and to give these two men an eternal place in the affections of a world of happy believers, and has shown that money and position can still have their uses when under the impulse of love. They were both councillors, rich men, members of the Sanhedrin, and in that class the Lord had not many disciples ; their pride would not even allow them to condescend to know Him, and certainly the greater part were hostile. They preferred their respectability to Christ, and so lost everything, Joseph and Nicodemus being excepted. These were the disciples of Jesus, and sooner or later must come out into the open for the assurance of happy fellowship with heaven, for heaven's approval of their conduct was based on their confession of Christ.

There were many who esteemed Him as a righteous man, or as a prophet mighty in word and deed, and others who hailed Him as the long promised deliverer for Israel, and as such rendered Him homage as the Son of God. There were, alas, others who regarded Him with indifference and contempt, and went so far in their wickedness by saying He was a profane Sabbath breaker and blasphemer, a madman and demoniac.

How may we account for this diversity of opinion ? Look where you will in the life of Christ you will find nothing but perfection. Is it not on the ground that to " the pure all things are pure, but to the unbelieving there is nothing pure ? " It has been remarked by another " that on all subjects touching on morality and religion we are affected according to our moral state," and no doubt this witness is true. On moral questions no amount of evidence can satisfy an unsound immoral state of mind, such is the dreadful nature of the poison instilled by Satan in the minds of the unbeliever in Christ.

Had the Jews been in possession of sound and honest hearts they would have had no difficulty whatever in reconciling His words with His deeds as being the long promised Saviour, and they would subsequently have reverenced Him. How solemn are the words of the Lord, " If only thou hadst known . . . . Your house is left unto you desolate."

Reverting back to Joseph and Nicodemus, it is the greatest possible encouragement for those who never knew the moment when they came to Christ to think that we are not informed how or when Joseph was convinced of the Messiahship of Jesus and so became a disciple. Of Nicodemus, we know that he came by night to Christ to get his hard questions answered and we believe that he had life as a result of that one interview. In the character of Nicodemus, there are some things over which we are obliged to mourn, such as his ignorance of true religion as seen in the Saviour ; then there was his timidity in the council (John 7. 50) when he had a grand opportunity of confessing his discipleship ; we are therefore glad to find that he puts away his false modesty at the last, and throws in his lot (virtually this is what it meant) with the despised followers of the Nazarene.

Someone has said that " THE TRUTH you will never receive unless you yourself are TRUE," and this is very soul-reassuring, for if you love Christ and the things of Christ you must of necessity be His for time and eternity, for did He not Himself say " He that is of the truth heareth my voice." In the history of Nicodemus we learn that it is not enough to believe on Him in a half-hearted manner if we are to be blessed. We have to confess ourselves as belonging to Him in the midst of a hostile unbelieving world. It was a severe test indeed for both Joseph and Nicodemus as they would be fully aware of the tremendous wave of opposition against Jesus. Through being in the council of the Sanhedrin they were acquainted with the resolution of the Jews that whosoever confessed that Jesus was the Christ should be cast out of the synagogue, which meant excommunication and all that that involved—practically death, socially and religiously. Being rich men and men of power the thought of losing honour, station and religious rights was not to be lightly entertained.

We read in the story of the rich young man who actually ran to the Saviour and afterwards went away sorrowful because of the price he would have to pay to inherit eternal life, how hard it is for those who are rich to enter into the Kingdom of Heaven. The present moment is unique in that at any time our Lord may return for His own to whom He has entrusted the privilege of confessing His name before Christ rejectors. He Himself said, " Whosoever shall be ashamed of Me and My words, of Him shall the Son of Man be ashamed when He shall come in His own glory, and in His Father's, and of the holy angels.

May it never be true of any of the readers of these pages " they loved the praise of men more than the praise of God "—an indictment from God which still stands against ordered religion without Christ as its centre.

We now would consider the very fine testimony and confession of both Joseph and Nicodemus which brought out their actual spiritual worth : brought to light indeed through the death of the Saviour (incidentally the death of Christ is the true touchstone of confession). Joseph, then a disciple of Jesus, and an honourable councillor (Mark 15. 43) went in boldly to Pilate and craved the body of Jesus for burial, and he, with Nicodemus (John 19. 39) as fellow confessor, wrapped the sacred body in spices and linen and committed it to its quiet resting place. How strange it all is. When the Blessed Saviour was living and ministering to the needs of others, many hearts beat for Him during His trial ; the judge himself agonised because he cannot acquit Him ; but not one voice is heard amongst that vast throng appealing on His behalf ; He must die.

When He is condemned even Judas is heard exclaiming " I have sinned in that I have betrayed the innocent blood." Then He is led away to be crucified amidst the tramp of the soldiers and the babel of voices of the mass of people ; many women are heard bewailing Him. Hanging on the Cross of shame the dying thief bears testimony to His innocence, His power, His coming Kingdom, and, above all, His grace and kindness. Whilst suffering there, all nature is in sympathy with that dread moment, the greatest luminary in the heavens hides its face as its Creator is dying. The centurion witnesses " Truly this Man was the Son of God " after Jesus cried with a loud voice and gave up the ghost. But now death having taken place the floodgates of love in the hearts of these two dear secret disciples breaks the barriers and surges onward to impel them forward in holy courage. They bury Him with reverent hands, and with feelings of deepest emotion render the greatest of all services. Happy privileged men who undertake a work denied to the heavenly host of angels. Seraphim and Cherubim look down with holy gaze upon these two devoted men whose conduct is so sharply contrasted with that of the apostles who forsook Him when He was apprehended, and who afterwards appeared to shamefully hide themselves. The apostles were not present at the funeral of their Master and Lord, only Joseph and Nicodemus with the women who came with Him from Galilee, together with Mary Magdalene and Mary the Mother of Jesus, who thus in silent sorrow became earth's mourners. Truly " He made His grave with the wicked, and with the rich in His death " (Isaiah 53. 9). He, whose first resting place on earth was a stable, and who, after He had entered upon His public ministry, testified that He had no abiding dwelling place, now finds His last earthly home in the tomb of a nobleman.

What a proof of His Messiahship is shown in the minutest details of the accomplishment of holy Scripture. Let us consider the bearing this burial in the rich man's tomb has upon the resurrection of our Lord. If the Saviour had been buried with the robbers in some common grave there would always have remained a measure of uncertainty attached to it, and our faith would have suffered immensely; but He was buried alone in a grave in which no other had been lain. Scripture is most emphatic on that (Luke 23. 53), together with other important details, as :—

(1) He was buried in a tomb hewn out of rock to which there was but one way of access.

(2) A great stone was rolled on the mouth of the tomb making it secure.

(3) His enemies recollecting that He had foretold His resurrection had obtained from Pilate a strong guard.

(4) They had sealed the sepulchre, and set the watch which would remain until the end of the third day. If at the end of the third day the body of Jesus was still in the tomb, then the priests' representations to Pilate that He was a " deceiver " would be true without further controversy, and His teaching a myth.

But on the very morning of the third day the body of Jesus was missing from the tomb. The stone was rolled away by divine power, the grave clothes indeed there, but instead of being thrown about in confusion betokening haste, everything was orderly, as indeed resurrection is, and the body of Jesus was not there. He had risen! An angel came down from heaven, rolled away the stone, and the mighty Conqueror over death and the grave, having laid aside His grave clothes, calmly steps forth, having the keys of death and hell. Hallelujah!

(Rolling away the stone is not necessary for resurrection of glorified Lord. He appeared later in their midst, " the doors being shut." The rolling away was to admit disciples, and to prove " He is not here.")

Low in the grave He lay,
  Jesus my Saviour!
Waiting the coming day,
  Jesus my Lord.
Vainly they watch His bed,
  Jesus my Saviour.

Vainly they seal the dead,
  Jesus my Lord!
Death cannot keep his prey,
  Jesus my Saviour;
He tore the bars away,
  Jesus my Lord.

CHAPTER XII.

THE LORD JESUS AS THE SUPREME SUFFERER.

" For God so loved the world that He gave His only begotten Son that whosoever believeth in Him should not perish, but have everlasting life."

—-John 3. 16

WE have in the preceding chapters considered at some length the characters of some of the creatures brought into contact with Christ. We now desire to consider the salient features of the Creator Himself brought into contact with His creature, man, in view of the suffering of death, and, with this end in view, takes upon Himself a flesh and blood condition that sin in all its totality might be for ever dealt with. In thus doing our Blessed Lord has glorified God His Father, and man has been eternally blessed through acceptance of the gift of eternal life freely offered.

Who is this Person who took upon Him this high office of dealing with the great sin question ? He is God and Man !

With unshod feet we therefore desire to

look into this wonderful mystery, which has been made known by the Holy Spirit sent down from heaven and set forth in the holy Scriptures. The word is so clear that the beloved apostle Paul says (2 Cor. 4. 3-4) : " But if our gospel be hid, it is hid to them which are lost : in whom the god of this world hath blinded the minds of them which believe not, lest the light of the glorious gospel of Christ, who is the image of God, should shine unto them."

Very reverently then as humble enquirers after truth we approach the Scriptures and we find that the Jehovah of the Old Testament is the Jesus of the New Testament come in flesh to save. We find that the divine nature of Jesus Christ was foretold by the prophets when speaking of the Messiah or by describing works and characteristics of God to be only referable to Jesus Christ.

Thus Isaiah writes (Isaiah 8. 14) : " And He (i.e., the Lord of Hosts) shall be for a sanctuary but for a stone of stumbling and rock of offence to both the houses of Israel." The apostle Peter writes : " Jesus Christ is *that* stone of stumbling and rock of offence." (1 Peter 2. 8).

In Isaiah 40. 3 we have " The voice of him that crieth in the wilderness, Prepare ye the way of the Lord, make straight in the desert a highway for our God." Matthew applies this expressly to John the Baptist, who was the forerunner of Jesus Christ (Matt. 3. 3). Unless Jesus be Jehovah God, this prophecy could not refer to John the Baptist.

Isaiah again says : " I am God, Unto me every knee shall bow, every tongue shall swear " (Isaiah 45. 22-23). The apostle Paul definitely applies this to Christ, the judge of all (Rom. 14. 9-11).

Later we have Zechariah, God's mouthpiece : " They shall look upon me whom they pierced " (Zech. 12. 10). John the Beloved Apostle, writing by the Spirit of God, says : " They shall look upon Him whom they pierced " (John 19. 37). The prophet says they would pierce *God* ; the evangelist informs us that they pierced *Jesus*, and moreover refers to this circumstance as a fulfilment of the Scripture.

Earlier on in Zechariah God Himself is speaking and He says : " So they weighed for my price thirty pieces of silver," and to domicile the happening links it up with " casting them to the potter in the house of the Lord " (Zech. 2. 12-13). Matthew says this is only referable in all its details to the

J

betrayal of Jesus (Matt. 27. 5-10). And also the Psalmist tells us about the Messiah proving His Deity. Psalm 2 says : " Thou art my Son, this day have I begotten Thee."

Paul takes up this prophecy and says in Hebrews 1. that this is Christ. Psalm 102, where the writer pours out His afflictions to God : " O my God, take me not away in the midst of my days." God answers immediately by asserting : " Of old Thou hast laid the foundation of the world and the heavens are the work of Thy hands " (Psalms 102. 24-27). Paul applies this again in Hebrews 1. to Jesus to prove that He was really God because He made the world.

Then the setting of Isaiah is remarkable. It has sixty-six chapters ; the Bible has sixty-six Books (thirty-nine Books in the Old Testament and twenty-seven in the New). Isaiah is divided into two parts. Chapter 1. 39 speaks of God and His rights ; Chapter 40. 66 speaks of a suffering Man for the sins of others and the consequent glorification.

So in God's Word of Truth :—Thirty-nine Books refer to God's rights creatorially and redemptively (Old Testament) ; the remaining twenty-seven Books tell us all about the Suffering Saviour and His coming glory as Man (New Testament).

When Jesus was here in flesh we hear Him

authoritatively saying, " I and My Father
are One " (John 10. 30). Then we have His
declaration of deity : " Before Abraham was
I am " (John 8. 58).

Scripture is full of the wonderful fact
that Jesus is God, which the writer begs the
thoughtful reader to study for himself (or
herself) in order to give assurance, faith
and joy in the heart. We can only touch the
barest fringe of this soul-satisfying truth here.
When Jesus was here we read : " He came to
His own and His own received Him not "
(John 1. 11). Greek scholars tell us that it
may be translated : " He came to His own
realm and His own *people* received Him not."
In other words His creation recognised Him
whatever His people the Jews did. Water
changed its nature into wine at His bidding ;
He stilled the raging of the sea without the
least effort ; He raised the dead with as much
ease as that of the commonest actions ; and
whilst His miracles were done with the fullest
concurrence of His Father's approval, they
bore no marks of dependence as that of a
creature to that of his Creator (for He was
manifestly God), but bore the fullest credentials of One who is Creator Himself.

Again we read such words as " Jesus
knowing their thoughts " and " He knew
what was in man," thus pioving that Emman-

uel (God with us) was present in their midst.

This then was the Holy One come in flesh to suffer and die. We have indeed the display in Him of incomparable worth surrounded by iniquity, oppression, injustice and cruelty, yet losing nothing of its lustre, but rather revealing a brighter glory in the background of sin.

The great purpose of His life was to finish the work His Father had given Him to do, and through it all, supremely meek and lowly, whose anger was the calm displeasure of justice and whose smile was the tenderness of infinite love. During the thirty and three years of His sojourn on earth His life was a continual burnt offering with its handful of fine flour : a Sacrifice, the incense of which has never ceased to ascend to the throne of God, and to fill Heaven with the most grateful fragrance. Even as a youth we hear His words : " Wist ye not that I must be about My Father's business."

His life was one of entire self abnegation, in His complete devotion to His Father's will. His tender love towards His disciples, His ever ready kindness and benevolence towards the world. The fruits of the Spirit found their full expression in Him, showing that Christianity in its vitalizing force can be worked out on earth, " But the fruit of the Spirit is love, joy, peace (three Godward), long-suffering, gentleness, goodness (three manward), faith, meekness, temperance (three selfward) : against such there is no law " (Galatians 5. 22).

Let us refer back to the 53rd chapter of Isaiah, where we find the Blessed Saviour predicted as the Man of Sorrows. It is there that He is shown as (1) suffering vicariously:— " He was wounded for our transgressions " ; (2) suffering relatively :—" Surely He hath borne our griefs and carried our sorrows " ; (3) suffering atoningly :—" smitten of God and afflicted."

Let us draw near with holy reverence and boldness.

(1) *He suffered vicariously* :—We had sinned against God : death and judgment were our portion and all the agony pertaining to such a state had to be known by Him experimentally as well as God forsaking Him at the end of such suffering. The agony of Gethsemane had to culminate in the agony of Calvary for our sakes that we might, by believing, be eternally free. " Herein is love, not that we loved God but that He loved us and gave His Son to be a propitiation for our sins " (1 John 4. 10).

(2) *He suffered relatively* :—The many waters of affliction and sorrow which over-

whelmed Him could not quench His love for His disciples. The reception of truth in them was so slow as to be almost imperceptible in spite of the clear wisdom of His discourses ; the number and splendour of His miracles; the purity of His life ; and the grace and gentleness which marked His conduct. When He knew the hours of His bitterest sorrows were fast approaching and when death and hell already threw their dreadful shadows over His soul, then it is that He forgets His own sorrows and turns to His disciples in the tenderest and most affectionate solicitude. He carries their sorrows for them and tells them of a glorious day right ahead when their sorrow would be turned to joy (John 16). *And this on the very night of His betrayal* !

(3) *He suffered atoningly* :—Who shall measure what He passed through when He poured out His soul as an offering for sin, consumed as a sacrifice by the fire of divine justice, yet in that consuming, completely exhausted the judgment that God might dwell with man in a new heaven and new earth wherein dwelleth righteousness, sin having been forever dealt with on the Cross ? We will now deal with what has been called " The seven words from the Cross," uttered by the Saviour :—

1. *Father forgive them for they know not
what they do* (Luke 23. 34). First, it is interesting to note that the word here is ἀφίημι
meaning "let off" and has no relation
whatever to eternal forgiveness. How wonderful this is, for when Jesus had recovered
from the painful shock to His pure and holy
body occasioned by the driving of the nails
into His hands and feet, His first thought
is for His enemies, and so His first utterance
became a prayer, and His first word " Father."
He had in His blessed ministry inculcated
the principle of forgiveness especially when
spite and hatred had caused injury, and
prayer in answer to persecution (see Matthew
5. 44-47), and here He completely vindicates
His Father's Word of Truth, and in that
vindication exposes His tender love to sinners.

His preaching and practice were one and
the same. In considering the characters of
the previous chapters our hearts have surely
burned with indignation at the treatment
meted out to this Sinless Saviour by those
who should have welcomed Him, coming
as He came with all the credentials of Heaven.
Had Jesus in this hour uttered one tiny word
of complaint to His Father against the conduct of His revilers, who could have ventured
to find fault with Him ? But as the sacrifice,
He tells His Father that they are committing

the sin of ignorance (they know not what they do) and that therefore there must be forgiveness for them. (Under the Mosaic law there was no forgiveness for committing the sin of wilfulness.) God's heart is now free to pardon, but to obtain that pardon we must repent and seek that pardon for ourselves. We may ask in passing, " Did God answer this prayer ? " Yes indeed, by giving forty years' time for repentance before destroying Jerusalem. The Lord Jesus is a forgiving Saviour. Let us run to Him.

2. " *To-day shalt thou be with me in Paradise* " (Luke 23. 43). Since the actual work of crucifixion would be left with the soldiers, it would appear—although by divine appointment we know—that Jesus was hung between two bandits. No doubt the incurable love of jesting inherent in the Roman in those days of supreme overlordship led the soldiers to think " Ah, here we have to put a superscription ' King of the Jews '—this King must have a guard of honour and so we will allow Him to have courtiers, one on each side " ; for the thieves were hanged immediately afterwards. But Jesus had come from Heaven to identify Himself with publicans and sinners, so this fresh insult became an added honour in His eyes. And it is not a little remarkable that the behaviour of these

two between whom He hung that day became a precursor of what has been happening since that day ; for then, as to-day, one was saved by confessing Him Lord, and the other lost by ignoring his sinnership and the Saviourship of Jesus.

Regarding the repentant robber, we borrow the language of another when we say " This great sinner laid on Christ the weight of his soul, the weight of his sins, the weight of his eternity ; and Christ accepted the burden." It is beautiful to think that in the blessed Lord's own personal agony His thought in turning to the thief was as ever, for others. The word Paradise παράδεισος is mentioned but three times in Scripture—(1) Luke 23. 43 : *For the sinner who repents* ; (2) 2 Cor. 12. 4 : *For the saint who serves* ; (3) Rev. 2. 7 : *For the overcomer who endures.* The Lord Jesus is a comforting Saviour. Let is cleave to Him.

3. " *Woman, behold thy Son ; behold thy mother* " (John 19. 26, 27). The word ἰδού means " see " and there are two thoughts connected with this expression of regard :— (1) Mary was doubtless a widow by this time, and this became the last act of filial piety ; and (2) there was the termination of the special relationship which brought the Saviour into the world ; but in His dying hour we

find Him concerned for her bodily sustenance. How it brings home to our hearts His perfect humanity in His care for others, for the Scripture was about to be fulfilled, foretold by Simeon at His birth : "a sword would pierce her own soul also." And what sufferings were hers ! Those hands that had once clasped her neck as a Babe, and had caressed little children as a Man, were now outstretched to save a world of ruined men ; but she could not wipe away the blood from these wounds as a loving mother would. John 19. 27 tells us that "from that hour that disciple took her unto his own home," and tradition tells us that they lived together twelve years in Jerusalem, and that he refused to leave the city even for the purpose of preaching the gospel as long as Mary survived. Only after her death did he depart on those missionary travels which landed him in Ephesus and its neighbourhood, with which his later history is connected. This third word is the end of the first three hours on the Cross.

The Lord Jesus is a loving Saviour. May we love Him in return.

4. "*My God, my God, why hast Thou forsaken me*" (Matthew 27. 46). This word ἐγκαταλείπω means "to leave entirely alone" and is mentioned but seven times in the New Testament, the same word being employed

in " I will never forsake thee " (Heb. 13), being the seventh occasion. It is a synonym with its corresponding antonym (forsaken, synonym ; forgiven, antonym).

This fourth word divides the two groups of sayings, and from this period there is darkness over all the land and into this mysterious darkness Jesus goes to deal with the great Sin question with a holy God ;— for three long hours He is to enter the arena alone ! Eternity itself will never penetrate through and understand what that interview meant to Divine Persons. We pause to bow our heads in holy reverent worship, for here time touches eternity : " Mercy and truth have kissed each other." The Lord Jesus is a sin bearing Saviour. Let us open our heart's door to Him *now* whilst time is still ours.

5. " *I thirst* " (John 19. 28). This particular word ὐιψάω is mentioned ten times in the New Testament, commencing with Matthew 5. 6 : " Blessed are they which do *thirst* after righteousness," and ending with Rev. 7. 16 : " shall hunger no more, neither *thirst* any more " ; has as its seventh word " I thirst," and beyond His physical sufferings we know that He thirsted to make His Father known. He remembered in the midst of His unutterable agony, and after the for-

saking, that there was a verse of Scripture tucked away in Psalm 69 and He would fulfil that.

Earlier in His sufferings the Blessed Saviour would not drink the stupifying drug, for with unclouded mind He would take up our cause with a Holy God and atone, the guiltless One for the guilty; but now the atoning work is finished, the darkness is passing for Him, and having suffered for others, He is free to think of Himself. Devouring thirst which was the culminating agony of crucifixion draws from Him this cry of personal need.

The Lord Jesus is a thirsting Saviour. Let us refresh His Blessed heart by sitting at His feet while He reveals the Father to us.

6. "*It is finished*" (John 19. 30). This is the word of victory, the triumphant end to all His sufferings on behalf of others. It is the topstone to His precious ministry. It means " to end " τελέω and is thus used eight times in the New Testament. It is the cry of a Conqueror. His great work on earth has now drawn to a successful close. Here it is interesting to consider what follows; we read " He bowed His head."

Earlier in His ministry He said to one who would follow Him " the Son of Man

hath not where to lay His head " (Luke 9. 58),
and the same word used for " lay " (κλένω)
is that used for " bowed." He as a homeless
stranger would only " lay " His head upon
a Cross of Shame in serving others, the work
accomplished.

The Lord Jesus is a triumphant Saviour.
If we come to Him *to-day* we shall share His
victory.

7. "*Father, into Thy hands I commend
my Spirit*" (Luke 23. 46). This is the last
word of the Saviour and as such it commands
our special consideration. The word
" Father " or " Pater " (Greek word πατηρ)
is mentioned 265 times in the New Testament, and it is noted that they commence
the first and last words on the Cross ad-
dressed to His Father. It is noted that the
fourth and seventh words are uttered in a
loud voice, and it is also noted that His
first thought is for His enemies : His last
thought for Himself.

Illustrious Sufferer, precious Saviour !
Reverently we approach the Cross and hear
the precious words and note that, apart
from the word " Father " it is a quotation
from Psalm 31. 5. How He lived in the
living atmosphere of the Word of God
through His life and now it stands Him in
good stead in His closing moments.

Death means a disruption of the tripartite parts of which human nature is composed. Spirit, soul and body are now handed over to His Father. Earlier soul and body had been, by life and sacrifice, given by Christ to His Father's will (see Eph. 5. 1), and now, the work having been accomplished, He commits His spirit to His Father. To quote from another, " Jesus knew that He was launching out into eternity ; and plucking His spirit away from these hostile hands which were eager to seize it, He placed it in the hands of God. There it was safe.

Strong and secure are the hands of the Eternal. They are soft and loving too. With what a passion of tenderness must the Father have received the spirit of Jesus.

The Lord Jesus is a faithful Saviour. Let us love and trust Him for time and eternity.

> Love that no suffering stayed,
>   We'll praise, true love divine ;
> Love that for us atonement made,
>   Love that has made us Thine.
> Love that on death's dark vale
>   Its sweetest odours spread.
> Where sin o'er all seemed to prevail,
>   Redemption's glory shed.

CHAPTER XIII.

The Triumph of Resurrection and Ascension.

" Jesus saith unto her, Touch Me not ; for I am not yet ascended to My Father : but go to My brethren, and say unto them, I ascend unto My Father, and your Father, and to My God, and your God."

—John 20. 17.

It is proposed to deal with this most important section in two parts :—Resurrection and Ascension, as they involve two different lines of truth.

1. *The triumph of resurrection.* That this is important as regards God's scheme in relation to future glory and final deliverance of this earth from the sad consequences of sin's invasion cannot be denied ; also its importance from the standpoint of the poor sinner's security and happiness is locked up in it.

The basis of the resurrection world gives the foundation of New Creation, as the apostle Paul assures us, " For the love of Christ constraineth us ; because we thus judge that if one died for all, then are all dead ; and that He died for all, that they which live should not henceforth live unto themselves, but unto Him which died for them and rose again . . . therefore if any man be in Christ, he is a new creature " (or as it should read " there is new Creation ") (2 Cor. 5. 14-17).

.But first let us consider the signs which accompanied the death of the Lord Jesus.

(1) " *The veil of the temple was rent in twain from the top to the bottom* " (Matt. 27. 51). This indicated to the priests who were then ministering, that God Himself had dispensed with the Jewish order of things and was breaking forth to reveal Himself in love and grace. This curtain of blue, purple, scarlet and fine twined linen speaking figuratively of the life of the Saviour in the four gospels now ended in death to enable God Himself to preach the glad news that the wall between Jew and Gentile was broken down and the worshipper may now draw near (see Hebrews 10. 19-22).

(2) " *The earth did quake and the rocks rent* " (Matt. 27. 51). If in the first sign the religious world without Christ was overthrown, in this we see the physical world as representing the hitherto stable system of Creatorial majesty and power, feeling the shock of resurrection ; the shock of a power which had never been known before.

(3) "*The graves were opened, and many of the bodies of the saints which slept arose, and came out of the graves after the resurrection and went into the holy city, and appeared unto many*" (Matt. 27. 52-53). This third sign means the overcoming of the unseen world, and corresponds to what we read in Col. 2. 15, everything being subjected to Christ. He entered into death's dark domain to release His people and to tell them that He " has the keys of death and hades." By His death and resurrection the Saviour had opened the gates of death to all the saints, for Matthew by the Spirit of God states it was *after* His resurrection the " bodies of the saints arose, etc." " Christ the first fruits, afterwards they that are Christ's " (1 Cor. 15). It was the certificate that, He having discharged every claim on their behalf, death had no longer any right to detain them. This becomes doctrinally the position for all believers, as taught by Paul the beloved apostle, who writes : " who was delivered for *our* offences, and was raised again for *our* justification " (Romans 4. 25).

So important is the truth of resurrection that we find the Godhead intervening. *Firstly* the Father's glory demanded it :—" Christ was raised up from the dead by the glory of the Father " (Rom. 6. 4)—*Paul's testimony*.

145

K

Then *secondly*, the Son :—" I lay down my life that I might take it again " (John 10. 17) —*John's testimony*. *Thirdly* the Spirit Himself :—" being put to death in the flesh, but quickened by the Spirit " (1 Peter 3. 18)— *Peter's testimony*.

All this truth is necessary to give settled peace to the heart, mind and conscience. And how attractive is the Godhead :—We have the *Father's bosom* ; the Son—*a " Lamb"*; the Spirit—*a " Dove "* in John's gospel (1. 18, 29, 32), so that we might be drawn by the cords of love, to call us away from the bondage, doom and misery of sin. Resurrection is everything according to the teaching of 1 Corinthians 15. Everything depended on the fact that He is risen. If He is not risen the preaching of His witnesses is vain, the faith of Christians vain. Not only that, but these witnesses are false witnesses, for they had declared, with respect to God, that He had raised up Christ from the dead. But God had not raised Him up from the dead, if the dead do not rise, and in that case their faith was vain ; they were yet in their sins ; and, moreover, those who had already fallen asleep in Christ had perished.

If in this life only, the believer has hope in Christ, he is of all men most miserable, for He does but suffer as to this world. But it is not so, for *Christ is risen*. Thank God, the One who had in His grace and love gone down into death to accomplish and display the deliverance of man in Christ from the power of Satan and of death, and to put a public seal on the work of redemption, also to exhibit openly in man the victory over all the power of the enemy, was now risen. In this Chapter 15 of Corinthians, we note also how Christ and His people are inseparably identified. If they do not rise, then He is not risen.

In a coming day, God acting in the Person of His Son, will call men from the tomb, for to His Son all judgment has been given ; but as to the believer, he has in Christ crossed the frontiers for ever. Sin, the power of the enemy, remains completely outside this new Creation. Adam and Christ are heads of two families. In Adam all die : in Christ all shall be made alive. Therefore we say : If in Adam then the person is still in that state of death : if in Christ then life and its blessed fruits are the enjoyed portion of the believer.

As belonging to the first Adam we inherit His condition, we are as he is, " Dust thou art, and unto dust shalt thou return " ; as belonging to the last Adam (Christ) though He was as truly Man as the first, He is from heaven and as participating in His life, we have part in the glory which He possesses as Man, we are as He is, we exist according to His mode of being, His life being ours.

2. *The triumph of Ascension* :—This equally important aspect of the truth commences with the deep-rooted and ardent affection of a heart set free from the dreadful misery of Satan's rule to that of the freedom of grace. Mary Magdalene, out of whom the Saviour had cast seven demons, appears first on the scene.

She is alone in her love : the very strength of her affection isolates her, and she misses her Lord. This forms the basis of her spiritual intelligence, for affection for Christ comes before intelligence in the things of God. She seeks Jesus because she loved Him, and so she comes before the other women, while it was yet dark, before the testimony of His glory shines forth in a world of darkness. It is a loving heart occupied with Jesus, when the public testimony of man is still entirely wanting. And we find that it is to this heart condition that Jesus first manifests Himself when He had risen. Mary Magdalene is ignorant in the extreme. She does not know that Christ is risen : so much so that finding an empty tomb she thinks that someone might have taken away His body.

But Christ is her all, the deep need of her soul proclaims to her—He is missing ; she weeps ! He is the only desire of her heart and without Him she has no home, no Lord, no anything. To this heart need Jesus answers, for it indicated the precious work of the Holy Spirit. As He calls His sheep by their name, so He says "Mary," and now she faces Christ and by that facing she received the revelation of a new relationship and new affections suited to that relationship. " My Father, your Father : My God, your God " : such is the position now.

What a triumph, and all based on " *I Ascend* " ! He must go to the Father in order that the Spirit might come down from a glorified Christ in dwelling the happy believer and making real and effective the blessedness of this relationship. This heavenly position of relationship and grace is connected with the present-day believers (i.e., those drawn to Christ during His rejection), for it would appear that by thus revealing Himself to the beloved remnant the old relationship is changed. He was not going to dwell bodily in the midst of His people on earth or to establish the Kingdom in Israel, for the word is " Touch me not," but by redemption he had wrought a far more important thing. He had placed them in the

149

same position as Himself, with His Father and His God ; and He calls them—which He never had and never could have done before—His brethren.

Until His death the corn of wheat remained alone.

Pure and perfect, the Son of God, He could not stand in the same relationship to God as the sinner, but in the wonderful, nay, glorious position which He was going to resume with His Father, and now as Man He could, through redemption associate with Himself His redeemed ones who are cleansed and made nigh. So He sends through Mary word of the new position they were to have and enjoy in common with Himself. As His friends He had prepared them for this before His death, but one thing had to be accomplished first before it could be effectuated :—He had to die.

But it was the same Person who loved them unto death who came into their midst bringing the proofs of love : " Handle Me and see that it is I Myself " on that first Lord's Day morning, and bringing them that which they could not have had before His death—" Peace."

The *triumph of Resurrection* is that our consciences are at rest because of the raising of the One who died for our sins.

The *triumph of Ascension* is that this introduces us to heavenly associations and relationships, which gives rest of heart, and a spirit of worship.

O Lord we adore Thee,
Blest Son of the Father,
Whose love without measure
   Surpasses all praise !
Thyself Thou hast given,
We know Thee now—risen
Ascended—in Heaven,
   Where on Thee we gaze.

Our Father, we praise Thee,
Thou source of all blessing,
The Son has revealed Thee,
   In fulness of Light.
We joy in Thy presence,
We worship before Thee,
In love and all blameless,
   In holiness bright.

CHAPTER XIV.

KING OF KINGS, AND LORD OF LORDS.

" And He hath on His vesture and on His thigh a name written, King of kings and Lord of lords."

—Rev. 19. 16.

IN this final chapter we reach the ultimate end of God's ways from Creation's dawn to the Millenial rest together with His purpose to place everything under the feet of His beloved Son, once called the Man of Sorrows. We have nearly reached six thousand years of sin and sorrow through Satan's introduction of sin, and now God Himself will have the last word, for one thousand years shall witness the glorious rule of the Lord Jesus, after which there will be the consummation of all (only mentioned in Rev. 21. 1-5), when God Himself " shall be with them, and be their God."

Before that happy event, He has destined that Christ shall have become supreme. We know that the whole world is waiting for this, and peace cannot be known on earth until that glad morning dawns. That someone must reign as the result of sin having broken down man's loyalty to God his Creator in order that there should be proper rule, is evidenced by the fact that in the Old Testament the word " King " is mentioned nearly *two thousand five hundred times* : in the New Testament over *one hundred* times. Then the word " Lord " implying authority is mentioned in the Old Testament over *five thousand* times ; and in the New Testament over *seven hundred* times.

It is also obvious that man in authority has been tested and found wanting so that God had to retire into His own counsels and bring forth in fulness of time His beloved Son. The four gospels give us in detail the kind of man who will ascend the throne whose wonderful pathway ends in death, because His inheritance came under Sin's bondage, and His sacrificial death has removed the liability.

It will be a wonderful moment when in that day of rule every person in God's universe will be able to look up and say " The Man on the throne died for me." It is because of His submission unto death that God has highly exalted Him and has given Him a name above every name. Heavenly, earthly and infernal beings will own Him Lord, to God the Father's glory.

Adam sought to make himself like God

by robbery when he was in the form of a man, and strove to exalt himself at God's expense.

Jesus on the contrary when He was in the form of God emptied Himself of all His outward glory of the form of God, and took the form of a man, then as man He humbled Himself. As God He emptied Himself and as man He humbled Himself and became obedient unto death, even to the death of the Cross (Phil. 2).

So God has highly exalted Him, for this is consistent with God's ways and principles : —" He who exalts himself shall be humbled, but he who humbles himself shall be exalted." The Man of Sorrows when here is now the exalted Man of God's pleasure, and as Redeemer and Lord of Glory shall yet fill all things. Let us bow down in adoring worship at this glorious truth. (His humiliation is a proof that He is God for God alone could leave His first estate in the rights of His sovereignty :—for a creature it is sin.) Every tongue is to confess that Jesus Christ is Lord to the glory of God the Father.

The whole world is seething in unrest, bloodshed, sorrow and wickedness—the only solution is the enthronement of the Saviour just as to-day the only rest for the soul is the indwelling in the heart, by faith, of Christ. Heaven will shortly open for Jesus to come forth as King of Kings and Lord of Lords. On earth He had been known as the faithful and true witness and this will not be lost sight of when He appears in overcoming power, treading the winepress alone.

We read before Heaven opens in Revelation 19 that " the testimony of Jesus is the spirit of prophecy " (verse 10), and from that we gather that it was ever God's intention to bring before us Christ's own overlordship. This is plainly outlined in every one of the sixty-six books in the living oracles of truth—the Holy Scriptures :—In

Genesis 41. Christ is seen in Joseph as Food Controller of the World.

Exodus 4. Christ is seen in Moses as Leader in authority.

Leviticus 16. Christ is seen in Aaron as the only One who could make atonement.

Numbers 6. Christ is seen in the Nazarite as the Supremely Separated One.

Deuteronomy 33. Christ is seen as King in Jeshurun (meaning upright people).

Joshua 1. Christ is seen in Joshua as the heavenly leader.

Judges 7. Christ is seen in Gideon as the Victorious Captain.

Ruth 4. Christ is seen in Boaz as the mighty Redeemer.

1 Samuel 5. Christ is seen in the Ark of God as the true God.

2 Samuel 2. Christ is seen in David as crowned in His people's affections.

1 Kings 4. Christ is seen in Solomon as being fully acquainted with Creation.

2 Kings 4. Christ is seen in Elisha as unwearyingly serving God's people.

1 Chronicles 4. Christ is seen in Jabez as dependent upon God entirely.

2 Chronicles 20. Christ is seen in Jehoshaphat as Leader in praise.

Ezra 7. Christ is seen in Ezra as the only recognised Scribe.

Nehemiah 1. Christ is seen in Nehemiah as leaving high office to serve Others.

Esther 6. Christ is seen in Mordecai as the One whom the King delights to honour.

Job 32. Christ is seen in Elihu as presenting true religion against false.

Psalms 8. Christ is seen by the Psalmist as set over all Creation.

Proverbs 9. Christ is seen as wisdom who has builded her house through sacrifice.

Ecclesiastes 9. Christ is seen as the poor wise man who delivers the city.

Song of Solomon 5. Christ is seen as Chiefest of ten thousand.

Isaiah 53. Christ is seen as the Man of Sorrows.

Jeremiah 2. Christ is seen as the Fountain of Living Waters.

Lamentations 1. Christ is seen as the Saviour weeping over the City.

Ezekiel 36. Christ is seen as One who gives a clean heart to restored Israel.

Daniel 7. Christ is seen as the Son of Man who has an Everlasting Kingdom.

Hosea 14. Christ is seen as the Lover of His people and the Healer of their backsliding.

Joel 2. Christ is seen as bringing in the day of the Lord.

Amos 5. Christ is seen as the Appealer to His people : " Seek ye Me and live."

Obadiah. Christ is seen as the establisher of Messiah's Kingdom.

Jonah 4. Christ is seen as coming back from the grave to preach repentance and forgiveness to the Gentiles.

Micah 4. Christ is seen as the Lord of the whole earth.

Nahum 1. Christ is seen as a Stronghold in the day of trouble.

Habakkuk 2. Christ is seen as filling the earth with the glory of the Lord.

Zephaniah 3. Christ is seen as obtaining praise and fame in every land.

Haggai 2. Christ is seen as the Shaker of Heaven and earth.

Zechariah 4. Christ is seen as the Headstone and Foundation stone of God's building.

Malachi 4. Christ is seen as the Sun of Righteousness.

Matthew 1. Christ is seen as the true Messiah King.

Mark 1. Christ is seen as the true Servant.

Luke 1. Christ is seen as the Son of God.

John 1. Christ is seen as the Lamb of God.

Acts 1. Christ is seen as the Man gone to Heaven.

Romans 3. Christ is seen as the Mercy Seat for the believer.

1 Corinthians 1. Christ is seen as wisdom, righteousness, sanctification and redemption.

2 Corinthians 3. Christ is seen as the New Covenant.

Galatians 2. Christ is seen as the Son of God who loved me and gave Himself for me.

Ephesians 1. Christ is seen as the One above all principality and power.

Philippians 2. Christ is seen as the Lord to Whom every knee is to bow.

Colossians 1. Christ is seen as the Creator of all things.

1 Thessalonians 4. Christ is seen as the One who will come *for* His saints.

2 Thessalonians 1. Christ is seen as the One who will come *with* His saints.

1 Timothy 6. Christ is seen as the blessed and *only* Potentate.

2 Timothy 4. Christ is seen as the One who will judge quick and dead.

Titus 2. Christ is seen as the One who gave Himself for us.

Philemon. Christ is seen as saying " Put that on Mine account."

Hebrews 8. Christ is seen as our High Priest serving us in Heaven.

James 1. Christ is seen as the perfect expression of law and liberty.

1 Peter 2. Christ is seen as the Living Stone.

2 Peter 1. Christ is seen as the One who has received from the Father honour and glory.

1 John 2. Christ is seen as the Advocate with the Father.

2 John. Christ is seen as the Son of the Father.

3 John. Christ is seen as the Truth.

Jude. Christ is seen as the Only One able to keep us from falling.

Revelation 22. Christ is seen as the Alpha and Omega—the Beginning and the End, the First and the Last. He is the Only One who will Universally Rule as God's Centre and Sun.

And in that Revelation 22 we have Christ's

thrice uttered word to His beloved waiting saints : " I come quickly."

We say " Amen. Even so come Lord Jesus." For He *must* reign, till He hath put all enemies under His feet. The last enemy that shall be destroyed is DEATH." (1 Cor. 15. 25-26.)

Lord Jesus, come, crowned with Thy many crowns—
The Crucified, the Lamb once slain
To wash away sin's crimson stain—
       Come, Saviour, come.
Lord Jesus, come ! Let every knee bow down,
And every tongue to Thee confess ;
As Lord of all come forth to bless—
       Come ! Saviour, Come ! !